W9-ATU-303

192 510 8480

LITERARY STUDIES AND REVIEWS

LITERARY STUDIES AND REVIEWS

BY

RICHARD ALDINGTON

Essay Index Reprint Series

BOOKS FOR LIBRARIES PRESS, INC.
FREEPORT, NEW YORK

First published 1924
Reprinted 1968

LIBRARY OF CONGRESS CATALOG CARD NUMBER:

68-16901

The author makes due acknowledgment for permission to reprint the following articles to the Editors of:

The Times Literary Supplement, The Criterion, The Monthly Chap Book, The New Statesman, The English Review; *and in the United States,* The Literary Review *and* The Dial.

CONTENTS

LITERARY STUDIES AND REVIEWS

LITERARY STUDIES AND REVIEWS

I

PIERRE DE RONSARD

THE vicissitudes of Ronsard's reputation through the centuries are of themselves a study in criticism. They interest us chiefly by showing the effect of a great French poet upon succeeding generations of his countrymen, but to some extent also by showing the unhappy results of literary spite and critical bigotry which for nearly two centuries concealed some of the most agreeable and musical of French lyrics. During the sixteenth century Ronsard was taken at his own valuation as the greatest of French poets. Ignoring or attacking their predecessors (as they were afterwards attacked or ignored), the Pléiade firmly insisted on their superiority over " barbarians " like Charles d'Orléans and Villon and agreed that Ronsard was their chief and the prince of French poets. Not even " divine Du Bartas " could shake this acknowledged supremacy. Sovereigns like François II, Charles IX, Elizabeth of England, and Mary of

Scotland flattered Ronsard with praise and rewards. His reputation spread even into critical Italy, for it was when Brantôme was buying a *grand volume* of Petrarch at Venice that a *grand magnifique* rebuked him, saying that in Ronsard France possessed a poet " twice as great as Petrarch." This excessive and almost universal admiration found its final expression in Binet's " Vie de Ronsard," where, among much other praise (which Bayle later snubbed as *chimères*), we find this—

Quant à ses œuvres, elles sont tant pleines d'excellence et de beautez, que nous les pouvons mieux entendre et admirer que les expliquer et imiter : et nostre Ronsard a fait si bien son prouffit de la profonde science de toutes choses, pratiqué si bien les grâces anciennes, et à icelles joint une telle fureur Poëtique, à luy seul propre, que depuis le siècle d'Auguste il ne s'est trouvé un naturel plus divin, plus hardi, plus Poëtique, et plus accompli que le sien.

Hyperbole could hardly go much farther ; a reaction was inevitable, but was so harsh and savage that more harm than good resulted for French poetry.

About the year 1600 a Norman gentleman named Malherbe (whose character was as sour and carping as Ronsard's had been sweet and enthusiastic) set out as the reformer of French poetry ; one day, chancing on a copy of Ronsard's poems, he began to strike out all the lines which displeased him.

Someone having remarked that he had forgotten
a few, Malherbe took up his pen and struck them
all out. That is the tradition, which is given for
what it is worth. Whether the tale be true or false,
the seventeenth century and its successor decried
Ronsard as much, as extravagantly as the sixteenth
century had honoured him. Soon the whole
Malherbe group was filling Paris with abuse of Ronsard and the Pléiade. Sainte-Beuve tells an amusing
tale about Mlle. de Gournay (an elderly and learned
lady who admired Montaigne and the Pléiade)
rushing out, *avec les yeux éffarés*, from a roomful of
poets of the new school of Malherbe. But all Mlle. de
Gournay's horror and protestations and good sense
were unavailing. Each generation of French poets
has made it a point of honour to assassinate its
immediate predecessor ; and assassinated the Pléiade
duly were. Malherbe's influence lasted two centuries. Bayle's article on Ronsard in the " Diction-
naire " is a masterpiece of perfidy and ill-nature.
He says not one amiable or even just thing, and
accumulates in his notes quantities of depreciatory
remarks on Ronsard. A glance through Bayle will
show how the whole pack of critics of the seventeenth century were yelping at Ronsard's heels,
sneering at his poetic genius, denying his learning,
and vilifying his character ; in all three of which
he was superior to most of his detractors. Even

13

Menage abused him. Even La Bruyère : " Ronsard et les auteurs ses contemporains ont plus nui au style qu'ils ne lui ont servi," and so on. And of course le Père Bouhours does not like him any more than Boileau, launching his venomous dart against Ronsard, who, " Réglant tout, brouilla tout." The voices were unanimous and unfavourable.

During the eighteenth century Ronsard's poetry fell into an obscurity similar to that which hid our own Elizabethan and Jacobean lyrists during the same period. Some vague conventional homage was paid to his name as a " father of French poetry," but it is doubtful if there was any revival of him similar to Thomson's revival of Spenser. A century ago, even, Ronsard was a name and little but a name in France. From 1630 to 1828 his poems were never once reprinted. In 1826, the Académie proposed as a subject for the " eloquence prize " a " Discours sur l'histoire de la langue et de la littérature françaises depuis le commencement du XVIᵉ siècle jusqu'en 1610." An ambitious young man named Sainte-Beuve began a " Discours " accordingly, but while writing it in the orthodox manner (i.e. by copying the remarks of earlier commentators) it chanced that he read a few books of poetry of the period. Sainte-Beuve was so struck by the " interest and fecundity " of this poetry

14

that he gave up the "Discours" and produced instead that generally admirable "Tableau de la poésie française au XVIe siècle." M. Pierre de Nolhac calls it a "timid rehabilitation," and certainly there is a note of timidity and apology throughout the book. The phrase "fumier de Villon" is unfortunate, and the young critic is profuse of genuflexions before the altar of Boileau. But it is easy enough for us who profit by his work and daring to depreciate Sainte-Beuve ; after all, he flouted all the pundits and the Academicians and said what he really believed. Sainte-Beuve's selections have remained the standard examples of the Pléiade ; it was Sainte-Beuve who exhumed "Mignonne, allons voir" and "Le temps s'en va" and "Quand vous serez bien vieille," and Du Bellay's "A vous troupe légère" and Remy Belleau's "Avril, la grace et le ris."

Sainte-Beuve's "Tableau" was avowedly written with the purpose of "attaching these studies of the sixteenth century to the literary and poetic questions of our own age." Nearly all fertile criticism is written with such an intention, no doubt, but the enormous vogue of the Romantic poets of 1830 contributed greatly to direct public attention towards the earlier poets. In spite of temporary reactions and sets-back the reputation and popularity of Ronsard have grown continuously through-

15

out the last hundred years. There is now a large body of literature, biographies, commentaries, and special treatises on some particular aspect of his life or genius. Numerous collections of the poetry of the Pléiade have been published ; every historical anthology contains some example of Ronsard, and only the other day a new Pléiade of lyrists announced that the influence of the sixteenth-century poet is still fertile. Between 1857 and 1867 Blanchemain published his collected edition of Ronsard, followed in 1887–93 by that of Marty-Laveaux, and in 1919 by the magnificent edition of M. Paul Laumonier. Still another edition for general use is being prepared by M. H. Vagany. To-day, three hundred and thirty-six years after Ronsard's death, M. Pierre de Nolhac, one of the ablest, most erudite and fertile commentators of humanism and sixteenth-century literature, can write—

Le gentilhomme vendômois . . . est une des figures les plus originales de notre littérature. Elle commence à être une des plus étudiées. D'excellents érudits s'y consacrent, etc.

Let us hope that the multiplied labours of the " érudits " will not destroy the interest of the " poètes," which M. de Nolhac notes also as a happy indication of Ronsard's present fame.

From this brief review of Ronsard's posthumous fortunes we turn naturally to his books. Two

aspects of his poetry may be glanced at : its effect
on the readers of the sixteenth century and its effect
on a reader to-day. We cannot, of course, hope
to recover that early flush of admiration and delight
which came to Ronsard's contemporaries as they
" discovered " him ; but to some extent M. de
Nolhac's delightful " Ronsard et l'Humanisme "
enables us to sympathize with this early enthusiasm
by telling us the qualities for which Ronsard's poetry
was then prized, the conditions in which it was
created, and the novelties it introduced into French
literature.

In this century we do not praise poets for being
learned. But in the sixteenth century the reverse
was true. Within limits the more learned a poet,
the more sedulous his imitation of the ancients,
the greater his renown. Ronsard delighted his
contemporaries and flattered national vanity by
expounding in French the new learning, the smooth,
nimble Italian manner and the " précision des
descriptions, l'épithète colorée et pittoresque, les
brèves images empruntées à la nature " of the best
Greek poetry. It is not quite correct to say that
Ronsard was " the first French poet whose work
bears a strong impress of the influence of classical
studies," because the study of Latin literature was
far more extensive than is generally supposed, even
during the Middle Ages. But Ronsard was the

B   17

first to imitate extensively in French the manner and form of Greek poetry. That is one great achievement of the Pléiade, and it was an end they deliberately pursued.

It is easy to recognize three steps in Renaissance poetry, the Italian, the French, and the English, in which learning diminishes and native genius increases as the impulse goes northward. The Quattrocentro and early Cinquecentro swarm with writers of Latin verse, and only a comparatively few poets, like Lorenzo de' Medici, Poliziano, Boiardo, and Ariosto developed poetry in Tuscan. (Of course it must always be recognized that if Italy led literature into the cul-de-sac of classical imitation, it also led the way out.) In England we had much crudity, but also much genius and comparatively few learned poets; the Renaissance was an immense stimulus to native poetry rather than a temporary and unfortunate check, as in Italy. In France we find the curious compromise between native poetry and classical learning which is so well exemplified by the Pléiade. French poets could not altogether persuade themselves that they were the legitimate heirs of Roman grandeur and Greek culture. France did produce excellent humanists who contrived to play with gusto the charming game which consisted in Latinizing one's name, collecting codices and collating texts, lecturing on the classics, abusing one's rivals, and writing to one's friends Latin epistles in the style of Cicero and the Younger Pliny. But in spite of this fact, in spite of the other fact that much of the best pre-Pléiade sixteenth-century poetry of France is in Latin, the great centuries-old tradition of French poetry, reaching through innumerable songs and ballads, *fabliaux* and *chansons de geste*, to the great epic of Roland, was too powerful to be wholly swamped by the vast wave of Græco-Roman imitation which swept across Europe. And so we find Ronsard reading Latin from his boyhood, studying Greek enthusiastically under Daurat in his manhood, and making that momentous decision to "imitate the Greeks in the vulgar tongue." It must not be forgotten that neo-Latin literature was then as popular as that in the vulgar, and far more esteemed by the learned. The fashion is now to scorn the whole of neo-Latin literature as pedantry, which is quite as foolish as to sneer at the great mediæval Latin poets as writers of "monk's Latin." There is a little pocket edition of neo-Latin poetry, published in 1555 by "Leodegarius a Quercu" (Léger du Chesne), which M. de Nolhac asserts was the very book in which Ronsard read the Humanist poets and from which he gathered many a hint for his own work. Italians chiefly fill the book, but there are some Frenchmen (Muret,

Michel de l'Hôpital, Du Bellay, Daurat), and also one Englishman, Thomas Morus. One turns over the faded pages of this quaint little book with a feeling of pity for so frail a relic of lost poetic glories, and a thrill at the thought that perhaps the very copy in one's hands might have been held by Ronsard. And, with the melodies of " Mignonne, allons voir si la rose " in one's mind, it is strange to come across these lines under the almost forgotten name of Angerianus—

> Pulcra brevi duras, rosa, tempore : forma brevique
> Tempore : sic formæ par, rosa, tempus habes.

But the tracing of Ronsard's debts to the humanists will perhaps never be finished, and in any case is a task for the commentator rather than the mere appreciator. The ample commentary of Marty-Laveaux contains some hundreds of cross-references to earlier poets.

Ronsard was immensely proud of his erudition and took every opportunity of displaying it. The " Premier livre des amours " alone furnishes numerous examples. The sonnet

> Ie ne suis point, ma guerrière Cassandre,

was even in the sixteenth century reproached as pedantic and burdened with mythology. All these earlier sonnets are filled with reminiscences of

20

Dante and Petrarch, of the "courteous love" kind—

> Amour rendit ma nature parfaite,
> Pure par luy mon essence s'est faite, etc.

Sometimes Ronsard happily imitates a Quattro-cento poet, as in the charming description, whose spirit seems to come straight from the delicate "Stanze" of Poliziano—

> Quand au matin ma Déesse s'habille,
>   D'un riche or crespe ombrageant ses talons,
>   Et les filets de ses beaux cheveux blons
> En cent façons en onde et entortille.
> Ie l'accompare à l'escumière fille
>   Qui or' pignant les siens brunement lons,
>   Or' les frizant en mille crespillons,
> Passoit la mer portée en sa coquille.

Another sonnet begins with a description of the atoms of Democritus; another echoes Ovid; a third Horace. A "Chanson" opens in the strangest manner that ever a song began—with a learned reference to the obscure Alexandrian, Lycophron—

> D'un gosier masche-laurier
>   I'oy crier
> Dans Lycophron ma Cassandre,
>   Qui prophétise aux Troyens
>   Les moyens
> Qui les reduiront en cendre.

The sonnet about reading the Iliad is, of course, well known (and is often censured as ostentatious), while in the " Elegie à Cassandre " Ronsard laments—

> Mais que me sert d'avoir tant leu Tibulle,
> Properce, Ovide, et le docte Catulle,
> Avoir tant veu Petrarque et tant noté, etc.

We must remember that all this display, which now seems pedantic and ill-mannered, was then received with complaisance by nearly all readers. It is now the fashion to praise an author for writing " as if he had never read a book "; but in the sixteenth century such a person would have been censured as grievously impertinent. To know, to increase knowledge, to make his culture as wide and as profound as possible was the ideal of each poet of the Pléiade. To begin the imitation of some Greek poet or some form of Greek poetry was a sure road to fame. One Lampridius, an Italian, first imitated Pindar in Latin. A glance at a few of these productions finds them extremely tedious; but in the sixteenth century Lampridius was included in all the anthologies and greatly praised by the humanists. It was, therefore, highly gratifying to Frenchmen and a source of praise for Ronsard that he should have been the first French poet to " Pindarize " in the vulgar tongue, the first to imitate the " Anacreontea " (published by Etienne as " Anacreon "), and the first to strive after the " manner of Homer." This

cause of immediate popularity was also in part the
cause of Ronsard's subsequent humiliation. The
first wild enthusiasm for Greek poetry, which
revered equally Homer and the Orphic Hymns
(Ronsard is very fond of these last because of their
complicated adjectives), Musæus and Pindar,
Lycophron and Theocritus, soon calmed down into
a more rational purism. The positive revelling
in Greek and Greek gods and Greek references which
is characteristic of Ronsard's Hellenizing period,
and which was so impressive to his generation,
struck later and more polished generations as mere
uncouth pedantry. But this early pedantry of
enthusiasm is to be distinguished from that cold
pedantry of the seventeenth century which froze
classical learning into an orthodoxy it has not yet
wholly cast off. From one point of view Malherbe
and his friends simply substituted an arithmetical,
thin-lipped pedantry for a pedantry which had been
joyous, expansive, generous, and quaint. Compare,
for example, the grace and thought of Ronsard's
amorous sonnets with the mere polish of Menage—

> Sous les ombrages verds la Nymphe que j'adore ;
> Ce miracle d'Amour, ce chef-d'œuvre des Dieux ;
> Avecque tant d'éclat vient d'éblouir nos yeux,
> Que Zéphyre amoureux l'auroit prise pour Flore.

Compared with the glorious *trouvailles* of Ronsard,
the beautiful snatches of song he was continually

23

pouring out, Menage and his generation, and Boileau and his generation, are (as lyrists) nearly as frigid, as correct, and as uninspired as the Italian prelates who celebrated "I Giuochi Olimpici" in "Arcadia" to the greater glory of the "Arcadi illustri defunti."

In attempting to define the pleasure a modern reader finds in Ronsard's poetry it is natural to take first the easy, if inaccurate, method of comparison with our own poets. The classic comparison (Sainte-Beuve originated it) is with Spenser. Now in some respects the analogy is a correct and even an obvious one. The rôle of Ronsard in French poetry is rather like that of Spenser in English poetry, inasmuch as they are assimilators, enrichers of the language, and a fertile source for new poets. Each in his own way domiciled and naturalized the new style of the Renaissance. Each passed through a period of Petrarchan sonneteering and each was profoundly moved by later Italian poetry: Ronsard by Poliziano and Spenser by Ariosto. But the resemblance goes little farther, especially when we recollect that Spenser was preceded by Chaucer and followed by Shakespeare in harmonious progression, and that Ronsard abruptly revolted from Villon and from Marot, and was himself in turn denied by Malherbe. Our pre-Restoration poetry gained immeasurably by possessing as fountain-head the bright, vivid, human genius of Chaucer and by a comparatively friendly evolution, so different from the traditional revolt of French poets against their predecessors. It is a significant fact that whenever our poets have taken to sneering at their predecessors, the quality of their work has fallen off. Renewal of theme and manner is always necessary, but the poet who takes up a tradition and carries it on to something nearer perfection is the poet who succeeds. Fortunate were those who inherited a vital tradition !

It is only in the more stately and sententious parts of his work that Ronsard is like Spenser, and even here the likeness is incomplete. The fragment of the Françiade is poor compared with the " Faerie Queene." The four books of the Françiade may have " introduced the Homeric manner " into French literature, but they are not at all fascinating reading. Probably the best passages are the Homeric simile of the gathering birds in Book I, and this meditation of Francus over his dead companions in Book III—

> Heureux trois fois les hommes, que la terre
> En son giron, mère commune, enserre
> D'un éternel et paisible sommeil :
> Si comme nous ils n'ont part au Soleil,
> Ils n'ont aussi le soin qui nous martire,
> Ny le désir de grandeur ny d'empire.

Ronsard comes nearer to an epic style in the famous "Discours des misères de ce temps," which, far from being a mere artifice, is deeply felt. The passages especially striking are, in the first part, those beginning—

> Ha! que diront là bas sous les tombes poudreuses
> De tant de vaillans Rois les âmes généreuses!

and

> Morte est l'authorité : chacun vit en sa guise :
> Au vice desreiglé la licence est permise.

And in the second part there is a magnificent denunciation of those who have pillaged, beaten, tortured, and left for dead "nostre France."

If Ronsard's efforts to endow France with a Homeric epic were less successful than Spenser's adaptation of the epic of Ariosto, it must also be admitted that Ronsard has written no ode which for stateliness, sweetness, and beautiful images can compare with the Epithalamium. In the sonnet Ronsard is both more fertile and more successful ; and when it comes to the Chanson, the Odelette, and the rhymed Epigram, then Spenser is fairly beaten, and we have to call in some of our purely lyric songsters like Lodge and Greene. Ronsard composed all his lyrics to the sound of music (it is no affectation when he talks of his lyre), and Spenser

PIERRE DE RONSARD

is no match for Ronsard in the light, tripping, delightful rhythms with their jingle of rhymes which were really the great contribution of the Pléiade. There are scores of such pieces in Ronsard, some running smoothly—

> Hé ! Dieu ! que je porte envie
> Aux félicités de la vie,
> Alouëtte qui de l'amour
> Caquettes dès le poinct du jour,
> Lorsque des aisles tu secoues
> La rousée quand tu te joues !

Sometimes they have a more dance-like and excited measure—

> J'entr'oy desja la Guiterre,
> J'oy la terre
> Retrepigner durement
> Dessoubz la libre cadence
> De leur dance
> Qui se suit follastrement. . . .

Sometimes they run to those tender, slightly mawkish diminutives which give the poems of the Pléiade so over-pretty a grace—

> Ma maistresse est toute angelette,
> Ma toute rose nouvellette,
> Toute mon gracieux orgueil,
> Toute ma petite brunette,
> Toute ma douce mignonette,
> Toute mon cœur, toute mon œil !

Sometimes running into the better mediæval tradition of pure song—

> Prenez mon cœur, Dame, prenez mon cœur,
> Prenez mon cœur, ie vous l'offre, ma Dame.

The verve, the sweetness, the music, the richness of Ronsard's lyrics at their best are only to be equalled by our Elizabethans—

> A fount it was that no sun sees,
> Circled in with cypress-trees,
>   Set so nigh
>   As Phœbus' eye
> Could not do the virgin's scathe,
> To see them naked when they bathe.

Spenser's nearest to this happy vein is to be found in " The Shepheard's Calender "—

> Bring hither the Pincke and purple Cullambine,
>   With Gelliflowres ;
> Bring Coronations, and Sops in wine,
>   Worne of Paramoures ;
> Strowe me the ground with Daffadown dillies,
> And Cowslips, and Kingcups, and loved Lilies ;
>   The pretie Pawnce
>   And the Chevisaunce,
> Shall match with the fayre flowre Delice.

Perhaps the Frenchman is not so much better after all.

PIERRE DE RONSARD

There is a " moral " difference between Ronsard
and Spenser which is very noticeable to the reader of
M. van Bever's reprint of the usually unobtainable
" Livret de Folastries." Through all Spenser's
poetry, in spite of occasional voluptuous descriptions, there is a chaste, almost Puritan, reticence.
Ronsard can Platonize and Petrarchize with the
best, but he is too much of a humanist to omit
endowing the world with some fresh variations
on the theme of the Priapeia. The " Livret de
Folastries " is a chaste work compared with some
of the creations of Beccadelli and Poggio ; but it
would scarcely have satisfied the scruples of the
author of " Let not one spark of filthy, lustful
fyre." And yet it would be easy to create a
wrong impression of the " Livret " by insisting
on a few passages which Ronsard himself sup-
pressed in his maturity. At worst they are no
worse than when

> . . . . a Grace
> Sprinkles another's laughing face
> With nectar, and runs on.

The " Sonnets pour Hélène " are a " pur
chef-d'œuvre du pétrarquisme français." They
belong almost certainly to the poet's later years,
and although he calls the lady " ma Pasithée "
and " ma belle Grecque," tradition asserts the

29

passion to have been quite harmless. There is something quieter and less fantastic in these later sonnets, which yield many beauties to a careful eye, but none equals the celebrated lines—

> Quand vous serez bien vieille, au soir à la chandelle,
> Assise auprès du feu, dévidant et filant,
> Direz, chantant mes vers, en vous esmerveillant
> Ronsard me celebroit du temps que j'estois belle.

The publication of these separate works of Ronsard is greatly to be desired. Ronsard's complete works are expensive and bulky, and contain a considerable amount of verse which is of small value. The anthologies tend simply to reprint the same pieces over and over again, so that Ronsard is generally known by a mere fraction of his achieved work. But a volume like the " Sonnets pour Hélène," or even " Le Livret de Folastries," does give an extensive impression of Ronsard's ability as a sonneteer or a writer of wanton and musical lyrics which cannot be obtained from a few poems or even from a whole volume anthology. The large collected editions, like that of Marty-Laveaux (whose text has been used throughout this article), will always remain the standard work for researchers and experts. But the tendency is to issue too many books for researchers and experts and too few for the intelligent reading public.

PIERRE DE RONSARD

If the best of Ronsard's works—and that includes
quite one half—were made more accessible, Ronsard would have many more readers, if fewer
commentators.

II

JOACHIM DU BELLAY

HOWEVER much we may dislike the idea, it is not possible to deny that there is a certain fashion in literature, especially in that vast body of literature which is good without being supreme. This fashion is to some extent set by the critical writers of each period, and one of the tests of great literature is that it eludes or overrides the changing of fashion. Something of this changing literary fashion may be discerned in our liking for the work of Joachim Du Bellay. To us he is a charming, if unequal, writer whose lightness, together with a certain fantastic melancholy and quaintness, make him attractive ; while to the sober eighteenth century, so pre-occupied with strictness of form and classical austerity, he must have appeared (if ever read) as merely one more specimen of " Gothic ignorance and barbarity." They might have forgiven him something because he loved Greek, but his conceits, his diminutives, his playful disregard of " moral instruction " must have left them sternly disapproving. To trace

32

out all the reasons and tendencies which caused this general change of taste would be tedious ; but in the particular case of Du Bellay we can point to Walter Pater's essay as one reason why this once forgotten French poet is now considered a necessary part of the reading of an intellectual man.

Pater's essay is the best possible introduction to Du Bellay ; for though he is undoubtedly inaccurate in some of his facts and rather too lyric in some of his praise, he has seized upon and expressed better than anyone the essential charm of this poetry. He has analysed better even than Sainte-Beuve the wistful home-sickness of the " Regrets," the modern feeling for " out-of-doors " of the " Jeuz Rustiques " and the Petrarchan delicacy of " L'Olive." In appreciation of these cardinal qualities which make up an author's genius there is little to be added to what Pater wrote ; his essay, in all that concerns the vital part of Du Bellay's art, remains unsurpassed. But since the early seventies, when Pater wrote his study, there has been much careful investigation of Du Bellay and his work, and we have now a much greater critical " apparatus " to bring into play for a clearer judgment of Du Bellay's achievement and contribution to European culture.

This large documentation is due to the labours

of Marty-Laveaux and Professor Chamard, who, especially the latter, have investigated Du Bellay's writings with learning and patience. M. Chamard's " Joachim Du Bellay " is indispensable to anyone who wishes clearly to understand the poet and his writings. Pater, who derived most of his information from Sainte-Beuve, was at some disadvantage and would probably not have ventured on some of his statements had he known as much as is now known. He misses, or only casually in the phrase " it was an age of translations " hints at what is perhaps the most significant thing in Du Bellay's writing ; for this later investigation shows that almost all his best-known poems are translations from Italian or neo-Latin authors to such an extent that one might almost inquire whether Du Bellay wrote any one good original thing except the " douceur Angevine." Du Bellay's significance is then not so much that he invented *poésie intime* (which is a debatable point), or even that he represents the last effort of mediæval poetry, but that he was one of the first introducers to France of the " new Italian manner," which was the manner of the Renaissance and the forerunner of so much modern literature. Through the Pléiade, in which Du Bellay is second only to Ronsard, French literature was singularly enriched. The old mediæval forms of the *lai* and *rondeau* and *ballade*, which

tended to make poetry merely an ingenious sort
of game, were abolished through them; they, like
Sidney and our other early Elizabethans, introduced an enthusiasm for Hellenism, and were active
in translating Greek and Latin poetry. Like the
Italians, they became deeply absorbed in this " new
learning "; they tried to write Latin poetry with
the other humanists; and it was rather through
comparative ignorance of the classic tongues in
France than anything else that they did not lapse
entirely into pedantry. The Pléiade, and Du Bellay
most of all, were unblushing plagiarists; and far
from confining their literary pilferings to the classics,
they extended them to the Italian writings of
Petrarch and his followers, and to the Latin poetry
of the humanists. They were necessary predecessors
of a new literature which would supplant the worn-
out mediæval formulas. Therefore, though we cannot find much of Du Bellay's which has not a foreign
original, we should be wrong to consider him a mere
plagiarist. All he writes has a strong personal
style; everything he borrows he transforms, makes
French. He did not so much copy as interpret
with sympathy, introducing to his countrymen a
new intellectual attitude which, after all, transformed
not only literature but life itself.

Joachim Du Bellay's existence was brief and
not over happy. He was the second son of Jean

Du Bellay and Renée Chabot, and was born at the château de la Turmelière, near Liré, in the year 1522. His parents died when he was very young; and he was left to the care of an elder brother (nearly twenty years older) who, far from indulging in "dreams of military glory" with his young charge, left him completely alone to run wild. The child made friends with "toutes sortes d'ouvriers et gens mécaniques" in the course of his wanderings, and generally educated himself. But this early neglect caused that weakness in health which ended his life so early. While still quite young he fell in love with a girl, to whom he wrote the "Olive" sonnets. The lady, insensible to the charm of poetry written by a penniless younger son, married someone else; and, to recover from his chagrin, Du Bellay went to the University of Poitiers, where he met several men who afterwards were of importance in his life— among them his future editor, Aubert, and Pelletier, secretary to the Cardinal Jean Du Bellay. Later he met Ronsard—accidentally at an inn, it is said— and studied with him in Paris. In April 1553, he went to Rome with his political relative, the Cardinal; and remained at Rome, with no great pleasure to himself, until 1557, when he returned to France. Three years later he died suddenly of apoplexy, and was buried near Louis Du Bellay, archdeacon and canon, "faisant jusque dans la tombe figure de protégé." He had friends, but quarrelled frequently—even Ronsard is said to have brought an action against him for plagiarism. He spent the best years of his life in a kind of elegant servitude ; and though in Rome he had a mistress, whom he celebrates in Latin verse as Faustina, he never seems to have found anyone to take the place of the lost lady of his sonnets. Poetry was his real, perhaps only consolation. In writing he could forget the worries and intrigues of his dependent existence ; in the use of his imagination he found the happiness life had denied him, and to poetry he confided his complaints, his nostalgia, and his affections.

It may be of interest to English readers to trace some of his debts to foreign literature, with a few quotations from originals which are seldom read now, and to show perhaps that his chief claim to be remembered is as one who helped to re-discover a lost tradition. The " Défense et Illustration de la Langue Française " does not come within the scope of this note, which is concerned with Du Bellay's poetry ; but since it has been extremely admired for its " delicate critical distinctions " and referred to as one of his principal works, it may be pointed out that large portions of it are translated from a similar work in defence of the Italian tongue by Sperone Speroni. It may no doubt be, as Pater says, "impossible to read without feeling the excitement, the animation, of change, of discovery," but if the " Défense " is read in that small edition published in 1908 by M. Pierre Villey, where Du Bellay's French and Speroni's Italian are printed in parallel columns, it is impossible to read without discovering that, lacking Speroni, the " Défense " is rather a minute volume.

Du Bellay did not apparently feel it necessary to acknowledge any indebtedness to the Italian for his " Défense "; but he writes with more candour in the preface to the " Olive "; " je m'adonnais à l'imitation des anciens Latin et des poètes italiens." The influence of Petrarch is considerable in these sonnets. M. Chamard has collected thirty-eight instances where complete poems or parts of poems are taken from the Italian. Even that sonnet which Pater quoted as a " perfectly crystallized specimen " of Du Bellay's art is an expanded version of part of a canzone of Petrarch (the twenty-fifth) beginning with the words : " Il di, che costei nacque, eran le stelle." Ariosto furnished matter for eight more ; and Pasquier remarks of another sonnet that it is " desrobé d'un Italien, et rendu fort fidellement en nostre langue." Whoever the original author was his name is not remembered ; and it is more than possible that others of the " Olive " series were taken from

Italians whose very names are now forgotten. The
following sonnet, one of the eternal commonplaces,
imitated apparently from the Latin of Giovanni
Pontano, will show with what charm of language
Du Bellay can dress the oldest *cliché*.

> Qui a peu voir la matinale rose
>   D'une liqueur celeste emmiellée.
>   Quand sa rougeur de blanc entremeslée
>   Sur le naïf de sa branche repose :
> Il aura veu incliner toute chose
>   A sa faveur ; le pié ne l'a foulée,
>   La main encor' ne l'a point violée
>   Et le troupeau aprocher d'elle n'ose :
> Mais si elle est de sa tige arrachée,
>   De son beau teint la frescheur dessechée
>   Pert la faveur des hommes et des Dieux.
> Helas ! on veult la mienne devorer,
>   Et je ne puis, que de loing, l'adorer
>   Par humbles vers (sans fruit) ingenieux.

It would be an endless task to follow Du Bellay
through all his translations, admitted or concealed.
He published one book called " Plusiers Passages
des Meilleurs Poètes Grecs et Latins " in which he
translated portions of Virgil, Lucan, Propertius,
Lucretius, Pontano, Fracastoro, Homer, Ovid,
Gallus, Columella, Horace, and Manilius. He translated the fourth and sixth books of the Æneid ;
and one of his famous sonnets, beginning " Telle
que dans son char la Berecynthienne," is a para-
phrase of Virgil. When Du Bellay imitates

39

a famous author he usually admits it ; when he imitates the Italian humanists he is often silent. His best and most quoted poems are taken from their works, of which the " Jeux Rustiques " and the " Antiquitez " alone will show many examples.

It is not possible to say what poet first sang of the ruins and dead glories of Rome, for the subject was popular throughout the Middle Ages. Pilgrims approaching the city sang songs like this :

> O noble Rome, mistress of the universe,
> Pre-eminent among all cities,
> Red with the rosy blood of martyrs,
> White as virgin lilies,
> We hail and bless you
> For all ages of ages.

The Renaissance, more occupied with pre-Christian culture, rather lamented the Rome of pagan glory than celebrated the Church. What is possibly the earliest of these Renaissance poems—the type upon which the others are founded—is that written in Italian by Baldassare Castiglioni, author of " Il Cortegiano."

> Superbi colli, e voi sacre ruine,
> Che'l nome sol di Roma ancor tenete,
> Ahi, che reliquie miserande avete
> Di tant' anime eccelse e pellegrine !
> Colossi, archi, teatri, opre divine,
> Trionfal pompe gloriose e liete,
> In poco cener pur converse siete,
> E fatto al vulgo vil favola al fine.

40

JOACHIM DU BELLAY

Così, se ben un tempo al tempo guerra
Fanno l'opre famose, a passo lento
E l'opre e i uomi il tempo attena :
Vivrò dunque fra miei martir contento ;
Ché se'l tempo dà fine a cio ch'e in terra,
Darà forse ancor fine al mio tormento.

This sonnet, which was famous in its day, was soon
multiplied into many poems by the imitative
humanists. Thus Giorgio Fiammingo made a
Latin version of it beginning—

En domitæ colles Urbis, sacræque ruinæ,
Quæ veteris Romæ nonnisi nomen habent, . . .

expanding the sonnet into sixteen lines ; and
another humanist, " il celebre Conte Niccolà
d'Arco," wrote another—

Excelsi colles Urbis, sacræque ruinæ,
Queis Romæ nomen vix tenuisse datum est. . . .

Castiglioni's sonnet and the different Latin variations on it were the origins of Du Bellay's " Antiquitez de Rome," the seventh sonnet of which is
a close translation—

Sacrez costaux, et vous sainctes ruines,
Qui le seul nom de Rome retenez,
Vieux monuments, qui encore soustenez
L'honneur poudreux de tant d'âmes divines, etc.

But apart from this, there are two other sonnets
of the " Antiquitez " derived straight from the

neo-Latinists. One is from the Latin of Lazzaro
Buonamico and the other from "Ianus Vitalis."
Buonamico is a traceable person, whose poetry
was reprinted as late as 1770 in Italy ; but investigation has failed to discover anything of Ianus
Vitalis except his poems. Since the honour of one
of Du Bellay's best-known sonnets belongs largely
to Vitalis, it is only justice to give his Latin its
due—

> Qui Romam in media quæris novus advena Roma,
> Et Romæ in Roma nil reperis media,
> Adspice murorum moles, præruptaque saxa,
> Obrutaque horrenti vasta theatra situ :
> Hæc sunt Roma : viden velut ipsa cadavera tantæ
> Urbis adhuc spirent imperiosa minas ?
> Nunc victa in Roma victrix Roma illa sepulta est.
> Atque eadem victrix, victaque Roma fuit.
> Albula Romani restat nunc nominis index,
> Qui quoque nunc rapidis fertur in æquor aquis.
> Disce hinc quid possit fortuna : immota labescunt,
> Et quæ perpetuo sunt agitata manent.

Du Bellay turned this into a sonnet, which has been
highly admired by critics and is to be found in many
anthologies of classic French poetry—

> Nouveau venu qui cherches Rome en Rome
> Et rien de Rome en Rome n'apperçois,
> Ces vieux palais, ces vieux arcz que tu vois
> Et ces vieux murs, c'est ce que Rome en nomme.
> Voy quel orgueil, quelle ruine : et comme
> Celle qui mist le monde sous ses loix,
> Pour donter tout, se donta quelquefois,
> Et devint proye au temps, qui tout consomme.

JOACHIM DU BELLAY

> Rome de Rome est le seul monument,
> Et Rome Rome a vaincu seulement.
> Le Tybre seul, qui vers la mer s'enfuit,
> Reste de Rome. O mondaine inconstance !
> Ce qui est ferme, est par le temps destruit,
> Et ce qui fuit, au temps fait resistance.

The " Antiquitez " were put into English by Spenser ; so that one Italian sonnet, expanded into a number of Latin poems, was still further expanded into a series of French sonnets, finally appearing in England as the " Ruines of Rome of Bellay."

What is perhaps the most delightful part of Du Bellay's poetry is contained in the little book called " Jeux Rustiques," written largely in imitation of the " Lusus Pastorales " of Andrea Navagero and Marc-Antonio Flaminio. These two Italians wrote Latin epigrams in imitation of those in the Greek anthology, and during the sixteenth century their work was largely read. Du Bellay translated about a dozen of Navagero's poems, giving them in the translation a strange lightness and beauty. Of these the most famous is the " Vanneur du Blé," taken by Navagero from an epigram of Bacchylides—

> A vous troppe legère,
> Qui d'œle passagère
> Par le monde volez,
> Et d'un sifflant murmure
> L'ombrageuse verdure
> Doulcement esbranlez,

J'offre ces violettes,
Ces lis et ces fleurettes,
Et ces roses icy,
Ces merveillettes roses,
Tout freschement écloses,
Et ces œilletz aussi.
De vostre doulce halaine
Eventez ceste plaine,
Eventez ce séjour :
Ce pendant que j'ahanne
A mon blé, que je vanne
A la chaleur du jour.

Navagero's Latin has already been quoted by Sainte-Beuve, but since it has a certain suavity of its own it may be quoted again—

Auræ, qui levibus percurritis aëra pennis,
Et strepitis blando per nemora alta sono :
Serta dat hæc vobis, vobis hæc rusticus Idmon
Spargit odorato plena canistra croco.
Vos lenite æstum, et paleas sejungite inanes :
Dum medio fruges ventilat ille die.

It is curious to note that, though one can trace Du Bellay's translations in so many cases, he does not seem to have touched Flaminio at all. Flaminio is in some respects the best of the neo-Latins, and it is odd that so active a translator as Du Bellay should have left him alone. The difficulty is to know when Du Bellay is translating and when he is original. Thus even the learned M. Chamard has stumbled sometimes. After pointing out how

Bembo and Navagero supplied matter for the " Jeux
Rustiques " he turns and praises highly as original
the " Bayser "—

> Sus, ma petite Columbelle,
> Ma petite belle rebelle,
> Qu'on me paye ce qu'on me doit :
> Qu'autant des baysers on me donne,
> Que le poëte de Veronne
> A sa Lesbie en demandoit
> Mais pourquoi te fay-je demande
> De si peu de baysers, friande,
> Si Catulle en demanda peu ?
> Et peu se peuvent-ils bien dire,
> Puis que compter il les a peu.

But Emilio Costa, writing on the Italians, says,
" Giocchino Du Bellay piuttosto che imitare, in
gran parte traduceva ne suoi ' Jeux Rustiques ' un
epigramma Ad Amicam. Vediamo i primi due
distici del Sannazaro "—

> Da mihi tu, mea lux, tot basia rapta petenti
> Quot dederat vati Lesbia blanda suo.
> Sed quid pauca peto, petiit si pauca Catullus
> Basia ? pauca quidem, si numerentur, erunt.

These quotations should bear out the contention
made earlier that Du Bellay ought to be considered
less as an original author than as one of those innumerable humanists whose enthusiasm and learning
created the Renaissance. Du Bellay was lucky,

because by writing in the mother tongue he escaped the contempt which quite naturally was poured on the later Latinists who had no enthusiasm but that of a repulsive pedantry. That contempt was extended to certain poets who do not altogether deserve it ; and it would be only an act of justice for those who have admired the Pléiade to recognize that they could have hardly have existed without the previous work of men like Pontano, Navagero, Flaminio, Sannazaro and the Amalthei. Even our own Elizabethan lyric poetry, so superior to the French and Italian, is yet much under foreign influence. Happily, a lack of learning kept the Elizabethans fresh and vital ; the truly conceited Italian manner did not strike root in this country. The poetry of Du Bellay is mid-way between the Italian and the English—fresher than the Italian, more pedantic than the English. But even Du Bellay in Rome could forget his books sometimes ; and (while awaiting the day when it is discovered to be a translation) we may admire as his this sonnet from " Les Regrets "—

> Voicy le Carneval, menons chascun la sienne,
>> Allons baller en masque, allons nous pourmener,
>> Allons voir Marc Antoine ou Zany bouffonner,
> Avec son Magnifique à la Venitienne :
> Voyons courir le pal à la mode ancienne,
>> Et voyons par le nez le sot bufle mener :
>> Voyons le fier taureau d'armes environner,

JOACHIM DU BELLAY

Et voyons au combat l'adresse Italienne :
Voyons d'œufz parfumez un orage gresler,
    Et la fusee ardent' siffler menu par l'air.
    Sus donc depeschons nous, voicy la pardonnance :
Il nous fauldra demain visiter les saincts lieux,
    Là nous ferons l'amour, mais ce sera des yeux,
    Car passer plus avant c'est contre l'ordonnance.

III

A SATIRIST AT THE COURT OF HENRI IV

THERE exists no portrait of the courtier who was one of the numerous satirists in the reign of Henri IV, the greatest among them being Maturin Régnier. This is not wholly unfortunate, because in reading these satires, which so often pass the vague limits of satire to become mere dirt or mere scolding, we can give a free range to fancy in trying to imagine what this extraordinary personage—a real Théophile Gautier " grotesque "—can have looked like. It would be positively disappointing if any portrait were to show him as different from the fantastic creatures imagined by Callot. He must surely have been thin, bony, and sharp, with pointed beard and moustachios, long legs, and large ugly hands, his face pale except for the nose—well lit up with copious visitations of sack and Alicant— the whole singular man dressed in tarnished finery and trailing a huge rapier. In short, the complete out-at-elbows French Catholic gentleman

48

of Henri IV's civil wars. Sir Walter Scott—who knew everything in French and English literature and history—has sketched a Scotch counterpart to Sigogne in the person of Sir Mungo Malagrowther—

Nigel started when he heard the high, sharp, and querulous tones of the knight's cracked voice, and was no less alarmed when he beheld his tall, thin figure hobbling towards him, wrapped in a threadbare cloak, on whose surface ten thousand varied stains eclipsed the original scarlet. . . .

Sigogne to the life! For, like Sir Mungo, this acid old French courtier loved to humiliate by his sarcasms young, self-satisfied, and less experienced men. We know very little really of Sigogne's life in spite of the thoroughness of recent researches, and the usual mass of " documents " collected give us the satirist's character far less vividly than the anecdote of Bassompierre preserved by Tallemant des Réaux in the " Historiettes "—

A son avenement à la Cour, c'estoit après le siège d'Amiens, il tomba par malheur entre les mains de Sigogne, celuy qui a esté si satyrique. C'estoit un vieux renard qui estoit escuyer d'escurie chez le Roy : il vit ce jeune homme qui faisoit l'entendu ; il luy voulut abattre le caquet, et, faisant le provincial nouveau venu, il le pria niaisement de le vouloir presenter au Roy. Bassompierre crut avoir trouvé un innocent, et s'en joüer ; il entra, et dit au Roy, en riant : " Sire, voicy un gentil homme nouvellement arrivé de la province qui désire faire la reverence à Vostre Majesté." Tout le monde se mit à rire, et le jeune monsieur fut fort desferré.

D   49

Sigogne was not unsuccessful in a worldly way, but he was very extravagant and died very much in debt. His full name was " Charles Timoléon de Beauxoncles, seigneur de Sigogne, Rocheux, Oucque, Saint-Simon et autres lieux." He held posts at Court, and was finally Vice-Admiral of Normandy and Governor of Dieppe. He was born about 1560 and died soon after the assassination of his master, on April 16, 1611. His tomb in the church of Saint-Rémy at Dieppe was mutilated in the Revolution (1791), repaired subsequently, and is now used by the verger to store his lamps.

Sigogne's verse is typical minor Renaissance satire ; that is to say, it is more gross than witty, has no moral objective, real or pretended, and is chiefly admirable for its variety and force of abusive and disgusting epithet. The greatest exponent of this satire in the satirical age of Henry IV was Régnier, to whom the better productions of these minor writers like Sigogne were often attributed. Régnier is far superior to his contemporaries ; he has more invention, more wit, more restraint, more genius, and he has the literary discipline, the power to organize his verve, which the other satirists of the age so palpably lack. But Régnier already shows the kind of Latinized satire which culminated in Boileau. Sigogne is more directly in the mediæval French tradition, that incomparably fertile school of satire which is not yet extinct ; but he, too, is not purely French. He had obviously dabbled in the *ordures* of the Italian humanists, works of incredible turpitude for which no equivalent is to be found in English literature. The writings of Bishop Hall and Donne, even of Marston, even the nastiest passages of Ben Jonson, Sir John Davies, and others less justified by genius, are mild and pure compared with the Latin satires of the humanists. Sigogne is not so purely depraved as the humanists ; there is something Gargantuan and burlesque in his nastiness. And both he and the Renaissance humanists have at least an excuse, though it may appear odd in modern civilization ; and that is, hatred of ugliness. We think ugliness of the person a misfortune that it is cruel and even base to denounce. Probably no modern can ever fully understand the Renaissance man ; certainly we cannot begin to comprehend him until we realize how important for him were beauty, magnificence, youth, splendour. To such men ugliness was an affront, a crime ; an uncomely woman far more despicable than a wicked one. Because they enjoyed beauty so much they revolted to an extreme of nastiness in depreciating ugliness. The moral satirists painted vice with the intent to disgust men with it ; these satirists painted ugliness for the same reason. Writers like Théophile de Viau and Régnier can hit off exquisitely beautiful lines and sometimes whole poems, if they wish. Unfortunately, the minor satirists were content with one vein, and rarely developed the other, more graceful, side of their genius which we should now prize so much more. Sigogne is particularly reserved in this respect, and it is a pity, for in one of his poems he shows a very happy fancy. He is describing a neat little lady in her hooped petticoat—

> Elle ressemble dans la bande
> De son petit vertugadin,
> Aux Damoiselles de lavande
> Dans les bordures d'un jardin.

A " Damoiselle de lavande," it should be explained, was a name given to tufts of lavender tied round the middle. The verse is wonderfully neat and the conceit is the kind of delicate fancy a refined modern poet would be happy to hit upon. Unhappily it is the one gem in the dunghill of Sigogne's otherwise satiric verse.

There are times when one questions whether Sigogne's work does belong to the category of " humaner letters," which theoretically at least interests all " honnêtes gens." Its prime motive —hatred of ugliness—is hardly comprehended now, and his diction is so hirsute, so ragged with obscure allusion and forgotten phrase, that some considerable knowledge of French is needed to understand it. He is not so difficult as Rabelais indeed, but then, how many Englishmen read Rabelais comfortably unmodernized? There are ten pages of glossary even in the last edition, which is meant for French students, who presumably are well acquainted with Rabelais. The curious and fantastic person of the author, in the rare glimpses we get of him, the rarity of his work, his place as an example of the eternal French *libertin* in an interesting period, are some excuse. The dealer in "historical comparison" would find ample material for his labours in Sigogne, for he must abound in reminiscences of old French and Italian satirists. But the true reason for reading him must be looked for in the works themselves, and I suggest that this is to be found in the copiousness and verve of his diction. Here we have that undisciplined vigour of imagination which struck positive terror into the chastened bosoms of pedestrian and uninventive writers of the Boileau school. Here we have old French in all its splendid crudity and homeliness and wealth of synonym and allusion, before it had been corrected by pedants. The ingenious flamboyance of Huysmans's diction is pale and effete compared with this astonishingly fertile growth. Their allusiveness may make the following lines obscure, but they possess some of that vigour which can only be fully appreciated

53

by reading the whole book. They are from a satire
" Contre une Dame Maigre et Sauvage "—

> O, le mal-heureux equipage
> De ceste grand femme sauvage !
> Des pelissons de son manchon
> L'on feroit bien un capuchon,
> Trois bottines et deux mitaines.
> Je luy donne, pour ses estreines,
> Un masque couvert de velours . . .
> Une biche, qui du bois sort,
> A ses alleures et son port,
> Et un sainct Crispin de boutique
> Les traits de sa medaille Ethique.
> Les joncs de son vertugadin
> Les chevenis de son Jardin
> Et les vitres de sa chapelle
> Ont autant d'embonpoint comme elle.

A sonnet " Pour un Soliciteur de Proces "
begins—

> Petit rat de bresil, qui vous a bottiné ?
> Où allez-vous ainsi, en robe de Guenuche,
> Les bras sur les roignons comme ceux d'une cruche.

He abounds in unquotable but marvellously insulting
denunciations of physical ugliness, of which the
following is a less intolerable specimen—

> Vostre embonpoint est d'escabelle,
> Vos bras, de casse et de Canelle,
> Vos dens, de crotte de Lappin,
> Et vos cheveux de regalisse ;
> Vostre nez faict en Escrevisse,
> Et vostre oreille en Escarpin.

A SATIRIST AT THE COURT

Vous êtes plus seiche que paille,
Douce comme une huistre à l'escaille ;
Vous parlez comme un sansonnet.

He has phrases that distantly recall Falstaff's abuse
of Prince Hal—

Et vous, manche de guiterne,
Souple comme un chat qu'on berne,
Guayne à mettre des couteaux,
Embonpoinct de sole fritte,
Visage de Trufle cuite,
Buandiere aux vieux draneaux ;

Image de la mort blesme,
Ne ressemblant qu'à vous mesme,
Sorciere allant au Sabath,
Medaille d'une Sybille,
Poire, pomme, femme, fille,
Rave noire, vieux cabat. . . .

Sigogne was never "weary of base comparisons,"
and even these extracts will show he constantly
repeated himself. Few will wish for more than a
few of his poems, but some day, when the French
catch our habit of anthology-making, Sigogne will
have his place among the "satyriques."[1]

[1] This anthology has since been published in four volumes by
MM. Fleuret and Perceau.

IV

L'ESPADON SATYRIQUE DE CLAUDE D'ESTERNOD

THIS book has been the cause of a curious dispute which led into error the famous bibliophile Paul Lacroix and Sainte-Beuve. It is worth mentioning, if only for the purpose of cautioning the reader against accepting the information supplied by either of the critics named when they are dealing with early French books. The error involved is simply that of the authorship of this curious and once very popular book of " invective satyres," whose title might be Englished as " The Satyrical Broadsword "—and, indeed, there is nothing of the rapier about it. The real author was Claude d'Esternod, but for many years this was supposed to be a pseudonym of a Gascon gentleman, Baron François Pavie de Fourquevaux. It is now happily proved that d'Esternod was a real person, did write the book signed with his name, .and that the Baron de Fourquevaux is an impostor as a poet, foisted upon the learned world as such by the ill-advised

56

piety of his descendants—which gives us little commentators a chance to score off the great critic Sainte-Beuve.

This poet's family was noble, antique, and vigorous ; it may be traced backwards from him to one Etienne d'Esternoz, who lived in 1132, and forward well into the nineteenth century. In fact, a M. A.-F.-C. d'Ésternod lives to this day in the picturesque old Château de Refranche (which was inhabited by the satiric poet three centuries ago), and is himself a poet. Claude d'Esternod's father was a famous soldier of Franche-Comté, and in 1595 he was commandant of Salins (on the Spanish side) during the wars between Philip II and Henri IV—a feat of arms greatly praised by the chroniclers. Claude d'Esternod, the eldest son of this military man, was born in 1592. Very little is known of his life. He married and had eight children. For the rest, MM. Fleuret and Perceau tell us, it is known that he became governor of a fortified town (like his friend and master, Sigogne), and was famous for the looseness of his morals. He is supposed to have known personally the satiric poets Régnier, Sigogne, Berthelot, and Motin, but it can only have been slightly and as a very young disciple ; for three of them were dead when he was twenty-one. The commentators hold that d'Esternod was a provincial rather than a Parisian poet, which would explain his continuation of a sixteenth-century *genre* into the seventeenth century. He was the author of several books, and contributed to the " Recueils " of the period ; he wrote little or nothing after he was twenty-seven. He died of the plague at Salins, in or about the year 1640. These are meagre details, but they are all that is positively known, and much raking of documents and learned acerbity went to the establishing even of these.

D'Esternod was the last of an interesting group of French satirists, who flourished contemporarily with our own Elizabethan satirists. They all observed to the full Bishop Hall's definition, or, rather, injunction—

> The Satyre should be like the Porcupine,
> That shoots sharp quills out in each angry line,
> And wounds the blushing cheeke, and fiery eye
> Of him that hears and readeth guiltily.

As a matter of fact, the innocent " cheeke " is more likely to blush at their words than the guilty ; and the only eye that is now likely to grow fiery at them is that of the literary purist, who will be shocked by their extraordinary verve. A lengthy comparison of these French and English satirists would be delightful to those who enjoy the quaint vigour and bombast they thought fit to assume. Unfortunately, this is impossible in a limited space.

One curious resemblance may be noticed, not to
a satirist, but to poor Stanyhurst's

> Of ruffe raffe roaring, mens harts with terror agrysing,
> With peale meale ramping, with thwick thwack sturdilye
>   thundering

in this monstrous couplet—

> Que d'un mau fin fio de ric rac renforcé,
> D'un boüillant vif argent soit son ventre percé !

The French satirists are rather more disgusting, and
certainly more obscene than their English confrères ;
the former quality they derived probably from
Italian predecessors, while the latter is inherent
in Gallic wit. The English pretend moral indignation
and do compass a certain bitterness. Their clumsy
vociferations sometimes reach a " rare invective
vein," but, especially in Marston, too often blow
up into an eruption of uncouth syllables, which
vapour of

> Ambitious Gorgons, wide-mouth'd lamians,
> Shape-changing Proteans, damn'd Briarians ;

or announce proudly,

> I cannot show in strange proportion,
> Changing my hue like a cameleon ;
> But you all-canning wits, hold water out,
> Ye vizarded-bifronted-Janian rout.

Unfortunately, most of the really gorgeous passages
in which d'Esternod rivals Marston are not quotable ;

they " something smack, something grow to ";
yet, by breaking off in time, the following passage
will give some idea of his burlesque, exaggerating
vein—

> Son gros nez me resemble une antique medaille
> De l'empereur Galba, ayant la mesme taille
> Qu'un manche de rasoir, sous lequel, aysément,
> A l'ombre du soleil se met un regiment ;
> Nez qui pourrait servir d'espouvantails tres-dignes
> A chasser les oyseaux qui se jettent aus vignes ;
> Nez d'argent de rapport, damasquiné, grand, long ;
> Nez de courde, cocombre, ou citroüille, ou melon ;
> Nez qui sent sa vendange, et superbe en son membre,
> Semble crier par tout ; purée de Septembre !
> Nez, le joüet des vents, comme en Mirebalais
> Les moulins ; né bronsé, couleur rubis balais . . .

And then it becomes too, too " satyrick " and French
for modern taste. There is something clownish
and puerile about this satire at best, something
which puts it into the Bartholomew Fair of literature,
a curiosity like the two-headed pig or the " maid all
hairy " ; the kind of literature to please those who
frequented Dame Ursula's stall and engulfed roast
pig and bottle-ale. D'Esternod's jests are sometimes
merely loutish, his coarseness abominable. We are
positively amazed at the things he imagines to be
funny, the situations he conceives as a moral censor.
The anecdote related in his 15th satire, " L'hipocrisie
d'une femme qui feignoit d'estre devote, et fut

60

trouvée putain," illustrates his curious sense of honour. He first describes the pious outward behaviour of his *dévote*, then relates how he found himself wandering the streets with no money and all his best clothes pawned ; a lady's-maid introduces him to her mistress's darkened room by mistake ; he pretends in silence to be the lover, and then, when the error is discovered (too late) and the " galante " lady turns out to be the *dévote*, he first is horribly rude to her, then denounces her " hipocrisie," and then blackmails her to the extent of ten crowns, as the price of his silence !

The subjects of D'Esternod's satires are varied ; they range from a light and typically Renaissance " La Mort d'un Perroquet que le chat mangea " to the piece of turpitude just described, from a " slap on the cheek " to the denunciation of a Protestant divine—for Claude d'Esternod was an ardent Catholic. It is amusing when one considers some of the horrors he laughs at, to read his scandalized invective against the marriage of two cousins. The best of his pieces is the first, " Sur l'ambition de certains courtisans nouveaux." It is comparatively free from the nastiness of which the poet gives us something too much ; it contains much moral indignation against the inevitable band of rising men who were pushing into the ranks of the old " gentry " ; and, like so

61

many of these early satires, wanders off into denunciations of any real or fancied abuse which happened
to come into the author's mind.   It does not quite
reach the summit of ungallant disparagement expressed in this couplet—

> Vous, de qui les tetins de peau de vieil registre
> Brimbalent sur le ventre en bissac de belistre.

but it has amusing lines on the swaggering " Gascons "
of the time—

> Ils font les Rodhomonts, les Rogers, les bravaches ;
> Ils arboriseront quatre ou cinq cents pennaches . . .

and—

> Quand ils sont attachez à leurs pièces de fer,
> Et qu'ils ont au costé (comme un Pedant sa verge)
> Joyeuse, durandal, haute-claire, et flambergé,
> Ils presument qu'ils sont tombez de Paradis. . . .
>
> Bragardants en courtaut de cinq cents richetales,
> Grignottans leur satin comme asnes leur cimbales,
> Piolez, riolez, fraisez, satinisez,
> Veloutez, damassez, et armoisinisez.
> Relevant le moustache à coup de mousquetade.
> Vont menaçant le ciel d'une prompte escalade,
> Et de bouleverser, cracque ! dans un moment,
> Arctos, et Antarctos, et tout le firmament.

D'Esternod is very quotable, and the quaintness
of his conceits is a great temptation to quote further.
Thus, when he is writing a tirade upon the theme

of " Pride goeth before a fall," he begins with these singular four lines which would have horrified the correct critics—

> J'ay veu des pins fort hauts élever leurs **perruques**
> Par sus le front d'Iris, et, tout d'un coup caduques,
> Arrangez sur la terre, et ne servir qu'au deuil
> D'un cadaver puant, pour faire son cercueil.

To describe a hanging corpse he says quaintly—

> Que si quelqu'un *gardoit les brebis à la lune*,
> Pendillant tout ainsi qu'un bordin vermolu.
> ("Bordin" is an old word for "bâton.")

In one of his poems d'Esternod announces that he is about to sing "Sur un vieil rebec plein de roüilles," and the image strikes one as a very apt description of his art—he is indeed a singer to a rusty old instrument. But the very ruggedness of his diction, the grotesqueness of his expressions, the sacrifice of everything to *verdeur* and vigorousness, make him particularly attractive when so many poets are merely graceful, amiable, and refined. When our own early satirists—so excellent of their kind—are neglected and even despised ; when there is an idea that satire is extinct, and another, almost worse, idea that " satire is not poetry," it would be absurd to expect a revival of these old French satirists. For all but a few enthusiasts they are

63

dead, and, as d'Esternod himself says, in an un-expected mood of depression—

> Sans y penser vieillesse arrive ;
> Ne plus ne moins qu'à une grive,
> Sans y penser la mort advient ;
> Et puis, quand vous avez des rides,
> Vous estes des vieux mords de brides
> Qui pour chevaux ne valent rien.[1]

[1] It is perhaps not incorrect to see in this a reminiscence of Villon.

V

SAINT-ÉVREMOND

SAINT-ÉVREMOND'S great gift is charm, the charm of an exquisite and amiable and rather *malin* personality. The slightest as well as the most serious of his writings possesses this cordial and fragrant charm. As we yield to his charm, smile at its pure and ever-present wit, applaud the common sense kept so light by good breeding, the antitheses of an elaborately simple prose, we understand why Saint-Évremond was so welcome a guest at Whitehall, why he delighted Buckingham and Waller with his conversation, why he remained always an affectionate memory to Ninon. It is to be apprehended that this charm is hardly appreciated by the readers of to-day as it was enjoyed by the best wits of the Court of Charles II. Mr. Whibley, of course, knows and appreciates Saint-Évremond; Mr. Frederic Manning has recently retold some of the well-known passages of his life; but in that Caledonian Market of literature, the Charing Cross Road, the works of Saint-Évremond

E
65

are a drug. They lie with Homer and Racine in
the sixpenny box. We have moved singularly
far from Saint-Évremond's own conception of the
intellectual life—

> Je ne trouve point de Sciences qui touchent particulièrement
> les Honnêtes-gens, que la Morale, la Politique, and la con-
> noissance des Belles-Lettres.
> La première regarde la Raison, la seconde la Société, la
> troisième la Conversation. L'une vous apprend à gouverner
> vos Passions ; par l'autre, vous vous instruisez des Affaires
> de l'État, et réglez vôtre conduite dans la Fortune : la dernière
> polit l'Esprit, inspire la délicatesse et l'agrément.

In life Saint-Évremond aimed at being the
" honnête homme " ; in literature he was the accomplished " amateur," an amateur who had the ability
of the master, whose taste regulated the genius of
Racine, whose approval delighted and consoled
Corneille in his old age ; a master of prose who
shunned the promiscuity of publication and only
on his death-bed arranged his writings and indi-
cated which of the pirated pieces attributed to
him were really his. If there is vanity of a
coquettish kind here, the wilfully assumed indifference of the *grand seigneur,* there is none of
the petty vanity of authorship, no thrusting of
his personality upon the world through the refined
medium of advertisement. There are no Saint-
Évremonds now ; the examples are extinct, the
mould is broken ; we have all sold " cheap what

66

was most dear." In England only perhaps some
remnant of the tradition of " honnêtes gens " still
remains, but how precariously ! It would be
ignorant or blind to deny that we still produce
excellent books, that we still possess a literary life
and a literary " movement " of interest and importance ; but we have lost the tone, the temper,
the charm which were so eminently characteristic
of Saint-Évremond and of the society he represented. Our most conscientious authors write for
themselves or for other authors ; if they venture
beyond these purely professional audiences, they
find a huge, inchoate public, not to be despised
indeed, but lacking the authority of a society of
" honnêtes gens " to correct gently their faults,
to console them by just appreciation. When Lord
Clarendon tells us of the friends of his youth, in
that series of incomparable portraits which occupy
the early pages of " The Life," he distinguishes
between the professional authors, like Ben Jonson
and Selden, and the " Men of more than ordinary
Eminence " like Lord Falkland, Waller, and
Chillingworth. The distinction is perhaps a little
arbitrary (Sir Kenelm Digby is among the first),
but it is sensible. And it is perhaps no great straining of truth to say that Waller's great influence
on our poetry (something of a puzzle, if one looks
only at his mediocre work) was due less to his

practice as a poet than to his authority as a refined judge.

This critical function of the "honnêtes gens," so important in the history of seventeenth-century literature, and so often overlooked, is very well appreciated by M. Maurice Wilmotte in his introduction to the selected critical writings of Saint-Évremond. One may say that he pitched upon the criticism of Saint-Évremond—not the most important or delightful of his writings—to form this volume, because he wished to bring out this aspect of society then. Naturally his arguments and examples are drawn from France ; but the same thing happened in England. We all know how the Elizabethan and Jacobean courtier worried and partly directed the stage by his importunate presence among the actors themselves. And so in France—

Il avait des juges, cela va de soi, mais ils étaient ailleurs que dans ces stalles d'orchestre où l'on prétend décider maintenant du sort d'une comédie. Ils étaient assis sur le " plateau," et c'est là, dans un contact infiniment plus proche (et parfois gênant) avec les acteurs, qu'ils écoutaient et échangeaient à demi-voix les premières impressions. Ces impressions, ils les communiquaient aux gens de leur monde, au sortir de la représentation (ainsi fait le marquis dans la *Critique de l'École des Femmes*) et peu à peu une opinion se formait, qui donnait le ton à la cour d'abord, à la ville ensuite.

Similarly the opinion of the two banished gentlemen critics, Bussy Rabutin and Saint-Évremond, was

SAINT-ÉVREMOND

eagerly sought by correspondents, widely spread
and commented on, and had an effect we can scarcely
realize to-day, when the only authority is the un-
certain and almost powerless opinion of critical
journals.

All this may seem rather a solemn preamble to
a few occasional pieces from the pen of a minor
author, but we have only to compare the " humaner "
criticism of Saint-Évremond with the slightly
pedantic " rules " promulgated by Father Bouhours
to recognize that the former still belongs to the category of universal literature, while the latter concern
only the literary student. Saint-Évremond's
criticism, so charmingly persuasive (" urbane "
Arnold would have called it), is purely the criticism
of aristocratic good sense, strictly limited, un-
imaginative, " correct." It makes no discoveries,
has no *flair* ; it refines upon a few principles, restricts
itself to a few authors. Saint-Évremond's culture
was purely Latin. He read and re-read his Latin
poets, but, so strong is his prejudice against what
is romantic, imaginative, fabulous, and " irregular,"
that he preferred Lucan to Virgil. He delighted
in Cicero's letters, and had a *tendre* for Atticus,
" the *honnête homme* of antiquity," as he calls him
somewhere. He knew Spanish, and delighted in
" the Homer of comedy," Cervantes. His Italian
was not good enough for him to appreciate the

niceties of its poetry (he knows nothing of Dante), but he had a just admiration for Machiavelli, whom he imitated. His preferences in French literature went to Montaigne, Malherbe, Corneille, and Voiture. He read Bossuet and Racine with admiration ; he mentions Théophile and Saint-Amant. He knew Epicurus through Gassendi and Bernier ; Descartes he knew and had conversed with. But he knew no Greek and little English. The great literatures of the imagination were closed to him. His remarks on the English drama are omitted by M. Wilmotte as of " slight interest " : to us they are extremely interesting as showing the taste of English society at the time, for Saint-Évremond knew nothing of English literature except what he was told by his English friends. He cites with approval Bacon, Ben Jonson, Hobbes, Waller, and Shadwell. But he says nothing of Shakespeare, nothing of Dryden ; and, look at it how one will, this is something of an enormity. " There are," he says somewhere, " a few old English tragedies, which would be good if they were altered," " en toutes les autres de ce tems là, vous ne voyez qu'une matière informe et mal digerée," And so that was what Mr. Waller and my lords Montagu and Buckingham, St. Albans and Arlington, Crofts and d'Aubigny thought of " Macbeth " and " King Lear " and " Coriolanus " ! Did not Mr. Waller himself

" improve " an old play called " The Maid's Tragedy "
in accordance with the dictates of reason and loyalty ?
So we can hardly blame M. de Saint-Évremond (as
Sainte-Beuve does) for not revealing Shakespeare to
the Continent ; Shakespeare was denied by those who
were not Ben's legitimate sons, but his bastards.
Among our comedies he praised " Bartholomew
Fair," and " Epsom Wells," and he produced a sort
of pastiche of " The Fox " under the title of
" Sir Politic Would-be." Whereupon Mr. Dryden,
smarting under the slight to himself, even more
than that to Shakespeare, wrote—

His examination of the Grand Alexandre, in my opinion,
is an admirable piece of criticism ; and I doubt not but that
his observations on the English theatre had been as absolute
in their kind, had he seen with his own eyes and not with
those of other men. But conversing in a manner wholly
with the Court, which is not always the truest judge, he has
been unavoidably led into mistakes, and given to some
of our coarsest poets a reputation abroad, which they never
had at home. Had his conversation in the town been more
general, he had certainly received other ideas on that subject ;
and not transmitted those names into his own country which
will be forgotten by Posterity in ours.

That is the other side of the question ; and yet I
make bold to say that even these terrific deficiencies
in taste do not invalidate the importance of the
audience of " honnêtes gens " in forming and keeping
a standard of good taste. Their influence in France
was generally for the good ; in England, after the

71

Restoration, they were too generally Frenchified by their foreign education to be sensible of the value of our own imaginative literature. In their criticism of English literature of intelligence they were doubtless right—at least, we have Arnold's authority for so believing.

But criticism was only a part of Saint-Évremond's literary activity. He wrote two comedies, some excellent "conversations," or dialogues, many delightful letters, numbers of essays, moral and philosophical, and quantities of verse. He wrote a political study, whose discovery during the trial of Fouquet caused his exile. Above all he excelled in "polite conversation." In his younger days he had a knack of fine satire (witness the famous conversation of the Maréchal d'Hoquincourt and le Père Canaye), which for delicacy and point reminds one of no less a genius than M. France. Indeed, this most able piece of writing causes one to regret exceedingly that Saint-Évremond wasted so much of his time and verve on trifles; had the novel been as respectable a form then as two centuries later, had M. de Saint-Évremond been a little less indolent, what a novel he might have left us, with his fine gift of style, his skill in dialogue, his penetration in reading character and his ability to record it! He persisted in regarding himself as merely a cultivated gentleman whose pleasure

it was to appreciate great writers and to "polish
his wit" by contact with their works; and we
are forced to acquiesce, though with immense regret,
in his aristocratic prejudice. Was there ever a
case of greater literary nonchalance than his refusal
to re-write the chapters of his most ambitious work,
the "Reflexions sur les divers génies du Peuple
Romain," after Waller had lost them in the confusion of the Plague and the Fire? And how lacking in curiosity this *bon esprit* was. There in the
first years of his exile was the old London of the
Tudors and Stuarts, with its bridge of houses, its
streets of timbered shops, its extraordinary moving
crowds, its multitudinous sects and characters;
and he says not a word of it. There later was
Shakespeare being played and widely read; Milton
publishing "Paradise Lost"; and Dryden engaged
in his combats with dullards; and he missed it all.
Certainly rather a high price to pay for an impeccability of *tenue* and an Epicurean tranquillity.

Among all the Epicureans of various shades of
opinion produced by Gassendi, Saint-Évremond is
perhaps the most delicate, the most genuine, and
the most attractive in his character and philosophy.
In one essay he divides men into "sensuels, volup-
tueux et délicats"; he was himself a "délicat,"
remote indeed from the gross orgies of the "goinfres,"
but equally repelled by what was austere, restricted,

and humble in Epicureanism. He is always pro-
testing against the ungodly habit of vegetarianism,
and he points out with cogency and wit that the
austere habits attributed to Epicurus well became
an elderly invalid of small fortune, but are not to
be desired at another period of life or in good health.
His Epicureanism was a kind of prudent refinement,
never allowing the pleasure of to-day to spoil the
pleasure to come to-morrow; the best of everything, but too much of nothing. As to friendship,
so strong a sentiment with the Epicureans, he
practised it with delicacy and disinterestedness,
though he did say that it was a species of traffic.
In love he was neither ardent nor constant, but
he seems to have kept the friendship of his mis-
tresses. The correspondence with Ninon is a very
delightful part of his writings. As to his relations
with the Duchesse Mazarin—the French commentators have exhausted the subject, though they
frequently omit the circumstance (rather disgraceful
to Saint-Évremond) that the duchess was brought
over by an English cabal to counteract the influence
of the Duchess of Portsmouth; and Saint-Évremond
knew it. Still, he was then a very old and a very
prudent man; he was an exile largely dependent
on the pensions he received from the King and the
Duke of Montagu; and then in that age of chivalry
they were less scrupulous about these things than

we are supposed to be. Saint-Évremond was a
complete sceptic, like most of the distinguished
people of his time ; he jests at Epicurus for his outward respect to the gods, but the Frenchman showed
a similar caution. His scepticism was never
obtruded, never harsh or wilful ; yet Montaigne,
Cervantes, Gassendi, and Hobbes are not exactly
the fosterers of conventional piety, even in a
character less sharp and self-indulgent than Saint-
Évremond's.

The charm of Saint-Évremond, then, is the
charm of a most accomplished gentleman, added
to that of a delicate writer, and again to that wistful sweetness so characteristic of the gentler sceptics,
Montaigne, and, in our time, Anatole France. As
a poet Saint-Évremond is above contempt, though
he never does more than versify an ingenious idea
or some philosophical thought. Yet, even here,
his gift of charm retains the attention ; and, to end
this all too slight appreciation of one of the most
agreeable exiles who have made England their
second country, let me give this sonnet, written
to Ninon de Lenclos, to show his occupations and
frame of mind in his wise old age—

> Passer quelque heures à lire,
> Est mon plus doux amusement ;
> Je me fais un plaisir d'écrire,
> Et non pas un attachement.

> Je perds le goût de la Satire ;
> L'Art de loüer malignement
> Cède au secret de pouvoir dire
> Des vérités obligeamment.
>
> Je vis éloigné de la France
> Sans Besoin et sans Abondance,
> Content d'un vulgaire destin ;
>
> J'aime la Vertu sans rudesse,
> J'aime le Plaisir sans molesse,
> J'aime la Vie, et n'en crains pas la fin.

VI

LA MOTHE LE VAYER

NOT the least interesting article in Bayle's colossal Dictionary is that under the heading " Vayer." It is true there is an intolerable deal of notes to a poor halfpennyworth of text, but anyone who knows Bayle knows that his notes are more important than his text. And how was it possible for the artful sceptic of the republic of Letters to overlook this patriarchal affinity ? Bayle has written of La Mothe Le Vayer with more than usual interest, and though he gets diverted in his notes upon a long and characteristic paper-chase about " les obscénitez," he gives us an agreeable picture of the old sceptic. And after enumerating all the real and imaginary advantages enjoyed by La Mothe Le Vayer, his commentator expresses surprise that the old man said he would not wish to live his life over again, and reflects that he is " un grand exemple du peu de bonheur que l'on goûte dans cette vie." To which we might add that he is also a great example of the caprice and

77

fragility of literary and philosophical fame. Sceptic though La Mothe Le Vayer was, and no unworthy predecessor of the immortal Jérôme Coignard, even his ataraxia might have been disturbed could he have foreseen how completely his reputation would dwindle to a bare mention in learned compilations, how utterly his works would be neglected by all save a few curious researchers. The last edition of La Mothe Le Vayer's " Œuvres " was in 1759 ; and the reprint of the " Hexaméron Rustique " in 1875 by Lisieux was certainly due to " les obscénitez " contained in that otherwise worthy performance. Yet we have omitted a most slender and yet most durable link with fame ; one of those accidents by which a man's name is preserved and nothing more, which was Cardan's idea of immortality. Thousands of people have read Le Vayer's name once in their lifetime, probably without attaching any individual to the print ; and that is when they read Molière's famous sonnet—

Aux larmes, le Vayer, laisse tes yeux ouverts,
Ton deuil est raisonnable, encor qu'il soit extrême ; etc.

In the pious labour of reviving the memory of the forgotten great we have not often so useful a peg as this connection with Molière.; let us make the most of it. La Mothe Le Vayer not only has the honour of being addressed by Molière in a sonnet, he shares with Gassendi (in the conjectures which form so large a part of modern historical criticism) the honour of having " influenced," perhaps partly educated, that great dramatist. It is certain that Molière knew and respected the old philosopher ; it is certain that when the dramatist died the " huissier sergent à verge au châtelet " found among his very small library " Deux tomes in-fo. du sieur de La Mothe Le Vayer." Unhappily there is no proof that Molière ever read them—and do we not all possess presentation volumes from learned friends which we carefully preserve, but never open ? Busy actor-dramatists have little time to read large philosophical folios ; whatever sceptical doctrines Molière professed were no doubt picked up in conversation, in the same way that Shakespeare learned everything that was worth knowing. There is one additional proof of Molière's connection with the Le Vayer household. M. Émile Magne has proved that the female to whom Molière read his comedies (a thousand-times-repeated anecdote) was not his housekeeper but Honorée de Bussy, a niece of the sceptic philosopher. And since Le Vayer's son, the abbé, was an intimate friend of Molière's, it is, perhaps, not straining conjecture overmuch to say that he owed a good deal to this household of cultivated people.

François de La Mothe Le Vayer belonged to an

old Breton family. An ancestor, who married a niece of the great Du Guesclin, settled in Maine in 1371. His father was Félix Le Vayer, Sieur de la Mothe (born 1547), *avocat au Parlement de Paris,* then magistrate, then *substitut des avocats et procureurs généraux.* François was the eldest of nine children ; he was born in Paris on August 1, 1583 ; not 1588, as is still commonly given by English authorities. Nothing seems to be known of his childhood. M. Tisserand (his biographer) skips the whole period 1583–1605 ; but he might have noted that Bayle says Le Vayer was educated by his father. This might account not only for his rare scholarship but for some of his peculiarities. In his youth he is reported to have indulged in " la débauche " ; he also suffered from " l'ambition de paraître " and " l'amour des richesses." The last two counts are his own admission ; his Latin poems and certain parts of the " Hexaméron Rustique " might be cited in support of the former, were it not for the " Lasciva pagina, vita proba," with which Bayle makes such play. But these were momentary errors of youth ; a " bon génie " led him into the company of the learned and revealed to him true philosophy. A " Socratic demon " ordered him to travel, and he appears to have indulged freely in that delightful occupation. He is known to have visited Spain, Italy, and England. He is very

learned in Spanish and Italian literature, and even
in the two dialogues now reprinted quotes Bacon
and Camden, and mentions the Royal physician,
Sir William Gilbert. One wonders—the specula-
tion is inevitable—whether he confined his attention
to the learned English authors who still used Latin
(Cambdenus and Verulamnus) or whether his
curiosity ever got the better of his philosophy and
dragged him over to the Bankside where sanguinary
popular melodramas like " Macbeth " and " Hier-
onymo " and " The White Devil " might be seen.
French visitors to England in the seventeenth
century imported with them a strong incapacity to
understand English literature.

There seems little or no evidence that Le Vayer
understood contemporary imaginative literature, but
he was remarkably open to all fresh ideas in philosophy and thought generally whatever its source.
This love of travel—which he shared with his great
master Montaigne—is highly honourable in Le Vayer ;
he lived into an age which settled into a kind of
insular perfection, that small perfection championed
by Bouhours and Vaugelas (with whom he had a
controversy), but spiritually he belonged to more
spacious times. His long life, stretching so late
into the seventeenth century, makes one think of
him as a contemporary at least of Corneille ; but
just as his speech contains fragments of the vigorous

F

old French of Montaigne and Rabelais, so his scholarship, his culture, his philosophy, his ample mind, and extended curiosity belonged to the more imperfect but more vigorous sixteenth century. No " Catholic Reaction " had subdued or smothered his ardent intellectualism ; he was a late but a very intelligent and lofty humanist.

In 1606 he occupied his father's office ; he did not marry until 1628—at the age of forty-five— so he had ample time for travel and uninterrupted study. His wife was the daughter of the learned Scotsman, " Adam Blacvod," whose name is so intriguing and about whose life the little that is known may be read in M. Magne's " Une Amie Inconnue de Molière." Marriage does not in the least appear to have modified his habits of study ; but the semi-Scotch bride seems to have inherited a certain feminine eloquence and tartness of expression which the whole body of Greek philosophers and modern commentators were inadequate to subdue. If he was not exactly henpecked in this first marriage it is clear that Miss Blacvod cared as little about Pyrrhonism and philosophy as the " auld fishwife " who swindled Mr. Jonathan Oldbuck. Bayle quotes very amusingly some of Le Vayer's solemnly depressed reflections on the married state.

In 1680 he published the first five of his dialogues

under the pseudonym of Orasius Tubero ; in 1631
four more were added. It is often asserted in works
of reference that these dialogues were published
posthumously ; this is incorrect. It is also quite
incorrect to say that his treatise on the education
of the Dauphin (Louis XIV) attracted the attention
of Richelieu. As a matter of fact he was well known
to Richelieu, at least eight years earlier. The reputation he derived from his dialogues, from his
erudition and travels, decided Richelieu to employ
him politically ; as early as 1632 he wrote a
defence of the Protestant alliance, and at least
five other pro-Richelieu pamphlets. Moreover, it
is hardly true to say that his " Considérations sur
l'éloquence français de ce temps " secured his election to the Académie Française in 1639. That was
due to his reputation as a man of learning (in which
he probably surpassed all the Academicians) and
to Richelieu's influence. The " Considérations "
are, as a matter of fact, rather an attack on the
Académie, since they traverse the opinions of
Vaugelas, one of the original members. Richelieu
intended to make Le Vayer tutor to Louis XIV,
and his pamphlet was—like the " Considérations "
—merely a public preparation for an honour which
had been already determined privately. But
Richelieu died in 1642, and the office was given
a man called Péréfixe. However, Le Vayer was

made tutor to the King's brother (afterwards the " Monsieur " of Saint-Simon), and later had considerable control of the King's education. Le Vayer's resignation of his legal offices in 1647 was clearly to be free to act as tutor to the Duc d'Anjou. In 1655 his wife died, and in 1664 his son. The latter event deeply moved the old man, and for some curious ironic reason he married again, Angélique de la Haye, who was forty years his junior, being a brisk young maid of forty. Le Vayer lived on to his eighty-ninth year, publishing several works in the years between 1664 and 1672. His last words, spoken to Bernier (popularizer of Gassendi's Epicureanism) were, " Eh bien, quelles nouvelles avez-vous du Grand Mogul ? "

La Mothe Le Vayer's work is voluminous. The Dresden edition is in fourteen volumes, and even then is not complete. His scepticism was probably the result of a comparative study of religions and philosophies. His investigations of the infinite differences in morals, beliefs, and religious practices make him an ancestor—and no despicable one— of the modern ethnologist. His dialogue on Divinity is not as interesting as the " Golden Bough," and, as Johnson said of the " Anatomy of Melancholy," it is " a little overloaded with quotation " ; but there is much to be learned from it. The twisting of several sayings of Saint Paul into a defence of scepticism is ingenious, a little over-ingenious in fact, for it would not deceive any Inquisitor. Both this and the other dialogues have that pleasant unassertiveness which is so great a charm in the genuine sceptics ; for after mountains of learning and subtle disquisition, he can turn to his interlocutor with—

. . . quelle témérité sera-ce à nous, si nous prenons le douteux pour le certain, et si nous défendons au jour d'hui avec pertinacité ce dont nous serons contraints de nous rétracter demain, ou de n'être pas plus raisonnables que ceux de qui nous nous sommes plaints toute cette aprèsdînée ?

VII

GUI PATIN'S LETTERS

THE pleasure to be derived from these letters is anecdotal and historical. They are matter of gossip rather than of criticism. What we are to look for in them is the expression of those details of human life, necessarily omitted by historians, which bring so clearly before us the day-to-day existence of men in other centuries, all the " little " things which pleased or worried or occupied them, as if they had not been under sentence of death like every other generation. The very remoteness of these interests to our own, which renders them indifferent or tiresome to the mass of mankind (and rightly), is an additional attraction for those who enjoy travelling in time, who extend their own lives by the imagination into the lives of others.

Sainte-Beuve found in Patin " a subject made to his hand " ; the two essays in the " Lundis " are admirable and definitive. The kind of analysis in which Sainte-Beuve specialized, attacking each author from a triple standpoint (as it were) of history, philosophy and literature, is there carried to its triumphal conclusion. Nothing more remains to be said. The reader is then recommended to consult the essays in volume eight of the first series of " Lundis," as the best possible introduction to the reading of Patin ; let us restrict ourselves to the much humbler task of tracing a few of the occupations of that rather choleric, wholly reactionary, and bourgeois doctor of medicine, Monsieur Gui Patin (very much " of the Faculty "), during the troublesome times of the Fronde.

The first letter in the collection before us is dated January 8, 1649. England is in the very centre of that earthquake which destroyed the old, vivid, coarse " Merry England " ; Charles I is at the foot of the scaffold. And, as always happens in these violent mutations of a great State, the shock is felt more or less severely by all neighbouring Governments. La Fronde is the repercussion in France of the Great Rebellion. Richelieu had left the whole State in almost perfect order, so that pretexts for the overt expression of bourgeois hatred for the aristocracy and the Crown did not occur until 1648. Mazarin was minister ; Emery the financial expert ; Broussel the popular hero ; Anne the " despot." The aristocracy, even to the Royal House, took sides according to personal ambition. I shall not sketch the turmoil of these months in Paris (available in any history of

France) except to recall that the legend runs: " Anne capitulated outwardly to the Parliament on the advice of Henrietta Maria, who apparently, had at length learnt wisdom." This capitulation, and still more the Queen's refusal to sacrifice Mazarin (as Charles sacrificed Strafford) saved the situation. That was in October 1648. But on January 6, 1649 (two days before M. Patin dates his epistle to " Monsieur Spon, Doctor of medicine," at the Place de l'Herberie, in Lyon), the Regent, the King, the Duc d'Orléans, and most of the Court retired secretly to St. Germain, and a *letter de cachet* was sent to the Parlement, commanding it to remove its sittings to Montargis. Condé, for the Crown, surrounded Paris with 8,000 troops ; Paris raised an army in opposition, commanded by the Prince de Conti and supported by the Dukes of Beaufort, Elbœuf, Bouillon, Longueville, and La Rochefoucauld. This quantity of nobles on the popular side seems to indicate that La Fronde was more a party intrigue than an insurrection.

But what has that eminent doctor Patin, on the verge of his election as " doyen de la Faculté," to say to his provincial correspondent, writing as he does in the exciting and unfamiliar circumstances of a civil war and a siege ? He begins, of course, with a note that he is safe personally, and then proceeds to discuss the then burning topics of the flight of the

Royal Family, the chances of conflict, of starvation, of an assault on the city? Not a bit. He begins with the leisurely assurance of the true *savant* to speak of those things which really matter—

Paris, this 8th of January, 1649.

Since my last, which I sent you on Tuesday, the 10th of November, the eve of Saint Martin, there has appeared a new book by M. David Blondel, minister of the holy gospel, intitled " Concerning the Sibyls celebrated as well by Pagan Antiquity as by the Holy Fathers," etc. Therein is much spoken of the vanity of the sibylline oracles . . .

So, with Paris two days besieged and learned physicians like to be taken for active service or at best somewhat scantily fed, M. Gui Patin is still so much master of himself that he begins with the (now unhappily forgotten) tome of M. David Blondel on that palpitating subject of the Sibyls. And before we arrive at such mundane and trivial occurrences as modern civil war, we hear of the death (by " hydropisie des poumons ") of that resolute and well-meaning man, Monsieur Nic. Héliot; of the ceremonies at the burial of this worthy, who left two quarters of a crown to every doctor who attended his funeral in a red gown and one quarter of a crown to each who came in a black gown and square bonnet, whereof sixty appeared, but the Faculty gave the money to the widow; of a letter from one M. Garnier; of the " worthy and incom-

89

parable gentleman," M. Gassendi, the Epicurean, " an epitome of moral virtue and the moral sciences and singularly well-seen in the mathematics "; of the speech of M. Talon ; of the death of M. Guenant ; of the evil part played by antimony in his last sickness, and of the " bons livres bien curieux " left by the deceased. And so we are gossiped along, with more medical small-talk and mention of a large book " De Infelicitate Litteratorum " (which might be added to at the rate of at least one folio a century), until at the end of the letter we hear of these unhappy political disturbances, due (it appears) to the inefficiency of Cardinal Mazarin. But Patin, like many another philosopher, is brave enough until the artillery opens out; " for my part I am a good servant of the King, but if my house is attacked I shall act as others do and defend myself as long as I can." Since his riches, like those of " le bonhomme Casaubon " were chiefly " libros et liberos," he was probably in no great danger.

The next letter is not quite so detached in spirit ; there was still no lack of food on January 25th, but the culinary preoccupations of the rationed begin to show through M. Patin's sententious prose . . . " il faudra prendre Saint-Denis, afin d'avoir aussi le pain de Gonesse, pour ceux qui ont l'estomac délicat et qui y sont accoutumés. . . ." The Queen has dismissed one of her waiting women, Mlle. Danse, and imprisoned a Canon, M. Bernage, for their pains in interceding for Paris. Songs and ballads and "force libelles," chiefly against Mazarin, prose and verse, Latin and French, are cried in the street, and Patin promises his correspondent a collection of them. What would it be worth to-day ? And the printers are out of work, except those engaged on "libelles," many of which contain such "méchant fatras" that a sort of censorship is established. On the 27th a "gros et infame partisan," named la Rallière, is imprisoned in the Bastille ; wheat and flour coming in by "divers entries" have "marvellously comforted" the faint-hearted ; Novarinus, author of "Omnium Scientiarum Anima," is a good writer, but Fabry de Castlenaudry is "un pauvre souffleur" ; an edition of Ocellus Lucanus, in Greek and Latin, is just published, and M. Patin has spent the sum of "trois pistoles en blanc" for Opera Omnia Spigelii, works now to be found only in the darkest and dustiest corners of old bookshops. Everyone is still in a "marvellous resolution" against "le Mazarin," even though the price of bread has gone up ; "nos bourgeois font merveilles," in the dangerous occupation of arresting innocent people at the gates of Paris. Everybody (on M. Patin's side) is "marvellous," and of course the war is the work of the Jesuits ; there has been a skirmish at Charenton, where M. de Chatillon was slain ;

much wheat comes into the city, but our doctor
becomes more violent daily in his attacks on
Mazarin—

Ne voilá pas de malheureux pendards, gens de cette qualité
et dignité se faire espions d'un maraud étranger, bateleur,
comedien, vendre, trahir sa patrie, son partie pour un Italien
qui n'est bon qu'à être chatré et à être pendu !

With such details the correspondent continues.
The new book of M. Gassendi on Epicurus is excellent ;
the Queen of Sweden has sent her portrait to Salmasius
and invited him to her Court, and he has replied that
for him Sweden is too cold and England too hot
(" for if the English have slain their lawful King,
what would they do to their enemy ? ") ; the " femmes
des Halles " went in groups four days ago to see M. de
Beaufort play tennis, and this Prince spoke familiarly
to one as " ma commère " ; the new edition of M.
Plempius's " Ophthalmographie " is not yet arrived
at Paris, but the " Jesuites sur l'échafaud," of the
P. Jarrige " s'y débite merveilleusement " ; there
is a famine in Rome, the Loire has overflowed, Mme.
de Chatillon has a son.

Pell-mell this heterogeneous mass of details, some
quaint, some unintelligible, some false, some true,
some mere prejudice, some professional, some general,
is poured out in a style already antiquated at the
period, but more agreeable in some respects than the
polished tones of later decades because of a certain

homely vigour, a rustic precision of imagery which put us very close to the pedantic old doctor. The scraps of Latin ; the contemptuous references to the "gazetier" (T. Renaudot, an enlightened and charitable man much persecuted by the reactionaries of his day) ; the admiration for Gassendi and Salmasius and forgotten chirurgeons ; the lamentations over a country house sacked by troops ; the delicious passage asking for a flattering dedication, "not for myself, but because it may one day please my grandchildren"—these and a thousand such strokes not only sketch very vividly Patin himself, but indicate a multitude of contemporary interests, give us the feeling of the time in a manner impossible in a work of more correct proportions. To the student of literature Patin is of small importance ; but for the amateur of life in all its curious contradictions and bizarre futilities he is delightful. A Parisian doctor writes gossip to a country friend who preserves the epistles, and after the lapse of centuries these letters entertain foreigners, whet their curiosity, initiate them into aspects of life which would otherwise have been quite forgotten. The very unconsciousness of Patin's style makes it so vivid ; had he ever felt that a distant posterity would read his letters, with what parade of pedantry, what awe-inspiring pomp of style, he would have sent them forth. Writing simply to his friends he makes us of the party, brings us his sympathy, so that we forget he was a cantankerous and rather silly old man and listen to his chatter as if it were the " song the sirens sang." Lively gossip, without self-consciousness, is an almost certain passport to fame—of a kind.

VIII

JEAN DEHÉNAULT

THERE is a pleasing illusion that genius triumphs over all difficulties, and that talent is always recognized and rewarded. On the other hand, M. Anatole France has revealed to us his suspicion that the greatest minds pass from the earth without leaving a trace of their existence. It is certain that talent may easily fail to reach fruition if conditions are unfavourable, that if some natures are stimulated to an obstinate energy by failure and neglect, others wither and become impotent under discouragement. This was clearly the case with Jean Dehénault, who was a man of considerable poetical gifts, which, if harmoniously developed, might have enriched French literature instead of leaving behind little but scattered fragments and indications of what might have been.

Dehénault had the misfortune to be born a little out of his due time, too late to have rivalled the wits of Henry IV, too early to have found supporters among the " Philosophes." He was a sceptic in religion at the moment when orthodoxy triumphed in France, and when literature, led by Racine and

95

Despréaux, followed religious orthodoxy. He was
of the unfashionable school, both in philosophy and
in poetry ; his life was not particularly happy, and
since he was poor, of plebeian birth and exceedingly sensitive, the vigour of his poetical talent was
half paralysed. To add to these misfortunes it
seems probable that such manuscripts as existed
at his death were destroyed by the pious fanaticism
of his confessor, for, like most of his contemporaries,
Dehénault made a last-hour repentance, though
from the account given, the poor old poet seems to
have been demented on his death-bed. Thus we
have only a fragment of his translation of Lucretius,
a work which would have given him an honourable
place among French translators had the whole been
as well executed as the few lines surviving. A fairly
large part of Dehénault's existing work consists of
piéces gallants of no great merit, except a long eclogue
in praise of Madame Des Houlières, which have
survived only because they appeared in various
contemporary anthologies. On the other hand, we
still have his fine sonnet in defence of his patron
Fouquet against Colbert ; his " Consolation à
Olympe," which was for many years attributed to
Saint-Évremond ; his versions of certain choruses
of Seneca, and his admirable elegy on fame, the
disillusioned but vigorous couplets of which constitute
perhaps his greatest claim to our respect. We must

add to this rather slight literary baggage the probability, persuasively advanced by M. Lachèvre, that Dehénault is the author of "Mélisse," a pastoral tragi-comedy which has frequently been attributed to Molière. Thus, if our melancholy Epicurean has left few traces of his literary talents, he has at least the somewhat remarkable distinction of having written a piece of prose which passed as the work of Saint-Évremond, and perhaps a play which men of taste have thought was Molière's.

Jean Dehénault, or D'Hénault, was the son of a Parisian baker, born at a date now unknown, but probably somewhere near 1611. His school career was brilliant; he completed his humanities at the Collége de Clermont, Molière's school. The social position of his family made a career difficult for the young scholar; and, after some time spent in the taverns of Paris, he visited Holland, England, and Sicily. It is interesting to learn from Dehénault that he was well received by King Charles, who would apparently have given him a pension had he consented to turn Protestant—

> Jusque dans Albion j'ai cherché ma retraite,
> Le Roi de la Tamise écoutait ma musette,
> Et ce Roi généreux eût été mon appui,
> Si j'avois servi Pan, comme on le sert chez lui. . . .

From Sicily Dehénault returned to France and sought a protector in the Prince de Condé. At the

Condés' house he met M. Des Houlières, husband of the celebrated Madame Des Houlières, who owed not a little of her literary abilities to the influence and lessons of Dehénault. In 1655 the poet received a small provincial office through the influence of Fouquet, and later he obtained a pension of twelve hundred livres. When Fouquet was disgraced Dehénault lost his office and his pension, but he continued to serve his patron with his pen. He was one of the first, if not the first, to defend Fouquet in a long and generous verse eulogy, and he attacked the successful rival, Colbert, in a bitter and contemptuous sonnet which was quoted all over Paris. It is said that Colbert was so struck by Dehénault's devotion to his fallen patron that he determined to continue his pension and sent the Abbé Gallois to inform him of this. The remainder of his life passed uneventfully. His insufficient means forced him to waste much time in purely hack writing, which has perished along with his translation of Lucretius. It is a curious coincidence that although Lucretius was translated in the seventeenth century by Molière, Chapelle, and Dehénault, all three have disappeared, no doubt through the destructive hands of over-zealous priests. He published anonymously a small volume of " Œuvres diverses " in 1670, unsold copies of which were re-issued in 1674 under another title. The keynote to Dehénault's character is his complete

indifference to notoriety, and it is generally the
case that an author who is too contemptuous of the
public, meets a similar contempt. Dehénault never
condescended to sign any of his works ; when his
" Consolation à Olympe " was attributed to Saint-
Évremond, it does not appear that he took the
trouble to claim its authorship ; and when Cotolendi
sharply criticized it as Saint-Évremond's work there
is no evidence that the amiable exile ever disclaimed
it. This remarkable dislike in Dehénault for publicity
is worth noticing ; the sentiment is always a sign
of certain superiority, even when it is not free
from affectation. In Dehénault it appears to have
been quite sincere. A man of great family, or one
remarkable as a soldier or statesman, may well wish
to keep authorship anonymous, lest, either through
his own failure or the too possible envy of others,
his writing serve as a weapon against himself.
Dehénault was a baker's son, practically dependent
on his wits for his livelihood. Yet he mistrusted
notoriety, with all the classic wisdom of M. Dubois,
practically as well as theoretically. It has been said
that he never troubled to sign anything he wrote ;
here are some of his exhortations to Madame Des
Houlières on the subject of " la Gloire "—

> On ne peut craindre trop d'estre trop estimée,
> Rien ne nous asservit comme la Renommée.
> On perd bien du repos pour faire un peu de bruit ;
> Et ce bruit ne vaut pas la peine qui le suit.

Pour moy je ne suis point la duppe de la Gloire,
Je vous quitte ma place au Temple de Memoire,
Et je ne conçoy point que la loy du trépas
Doive épargner mon nom, et ne m'épargner pas . . .

Qui jouira pour moy de ces honneurs postumes,
Quand je ne seray plus qu'un amas de volumes ?
Ce qui reste des morts reste pour les vivans,
Et va mourir comme eux dans les ages suivans.
Ainsi du grand Homère, ainsi du grand Virgile,
L'éloquence et la gloire eurent un sort fragile.
L'une et l'autre nous touche, et ne les touche plus.
Les grands titres pour eux sont titres superflus.
Tandis qu'on les admire, et tandis qu'on les loue,
L'impitoyable Temps de leurs œuvres se joue.
Nous regrettons déjà ceux qu'il nous à ravis ;
Et des autres un jour ceux-là seront suivis.
Un siècle d'ignorans, un siècle de barbares,
Peut-estre étouffera des ouvrages si rares . . . .

The theme was a favourite with the poet, and
suited his mood of cheerful pessimism, which contents
itself with what it has rather because it dreads the
envious gods may send something worse, than because
it rises from any expansive feeling of gratitude.
Thus, in his " Discours à M. L'Abbé de la Chambre,"
he sets off immediately on the same theme with
extraordinary poetic ability—

Oui, La Chambre, il est vrai, j'aime l'obscurité :
J'en chéris les douceurs et la tranquillité ;
J'aime l'état paisible ou le Ciel m'a fait naître,
Et c'est assez pour moi si je puis me connaître.
Aussi, pourquoi forcer les destins et mon sort ?
Pourquoi courir les mers, si je suis dans le port ?

JEAN DEHÉNAULT

Pourquoi, me voyant libre, avouer pour maitresse
L'aveugle, l'inconstante, et l'injuste Déesse ?
Pourquoi rompre le joug ou je semble attaché,
Pour en subir un autre ou je sois moins caché ?
Qu'importe que nos jours, quand ils coulent sans peine,
Soient des Parques là-bas filés d'or ou de laine !

"The grapes are sour," remarks his latest editor.
But he is surely mistaken. Dehénault was a dis-
couraged but not a disappointed man ; he was over-
sensitive but not bitter. The unfavourable nature
of his circumstances undoubtedly prevented the full
growth of his talents, but did not sour him. He
was marked by "gentle melancholy" from his youth
up ; the stoicism of Seneca, the epicureanism of
Lucretius were the conceptions of life to which he
naturally turned. Dehénault had recaptured something of the ancient wisdom of the classics, and in
his excellent translations one feels the emotion and
conviction of the translator—

On a vu les Mortels trainer long-tems leur vie
Sous la Religion durement asservie ;
Long-tems du haut du Ciel ce fantôme effrayant,
A lancée sur la terre un regard foudroyant ;
Mais un Grec le premier plein d'une sage audace
L'osa voir d'un œil fixe, et l'insulter en face.

There is a stir in the translator's words which
shows how profoundly he was moved by his immortal
original. Similarly the resigned pessimism of Seneca
moved him. Where M. Lachèvre is wrong in his

estimate of Dehénault is in his assumption that
scepticism of itself implies spiritual sterility, a petty
vanity, and a life of persistent debauchery. He
does not sufficiently appreciate the fact that the
yearning and delicate scepticism of a man like
Dehénault is as purely spiritual as the mystic's
ecstatic yearning. What is alone disgraceful is
spiritual indifference, the cold brutality of ignoran'
materialism, the cold formality of dull orthodoxy.
But Dehénault was guilty of neither of these ; he was
a poet and a scholar, a philosopher and an honest
man. And if his own age failed to understand him
and his poetry, we may at least try to do better.
Among all the scores of seventeenth-century minor
authors, he is certainly one of the most attractive
and genuine.

IX

COWLEY AND THE FRENCH EPICUREANS

IT is regrettable that we do not possess more of Cowley's prose. Apart from the "Discourse Concerning the Government of Oliver Cromwell," which is languid in manner and petulant in tone, all Cowley's prose is pleasing, whether it be the rapid popular speech of "The Cutter of Coleman Street," the "easy familiarity" of his letter-writing, or the urbane sententiousness of his "Essays." Unhappily, Cowley did not live to complete the "Essays" as he had planned, and those we have are more burdened with citation and translation than modern taste allows ; though, if this be a fault, it is one shared with Montaigne and Bacon. "The Cutter of Coleman Street," for all its briskness and raciness, obtains little praise nowadays, perhaps from the fashion which makes English drama fall with King Charles's head. What is greatly to be lamented is the loss of Cowley's letters, only a few of which (it appears) are preserved, and one of those because it chanced to gratify Johnson's spleen against a country life. We owe this loss principally to " the courtly Sprat," whose own words may be used in evidence against him—

This familiar way of verse puts me in mind of one kind of Prose wherein Mr. *Cowley* was excellent ; and that is his Letters to his private *Friends*. In these he always express'd the Native tenderness and innocent gayety of his Mind. I think, Sir, you and I have the greatest Collection of this sort. But I know you agree with me, that nothing of this Nature should be published : And herein you have always consented to approve of the modest Judgment of our Countrymen above the practice of some of our Neighbours, and chiefly of the French.

Sprat was Cowley's literary executor and editor, but whether he destroyed Cowley's letters or whether they are yet extant does not appear. In spite of our own and Dr. Sprat's objections to literary gossip, he seems to have been too scrupulous ; a collection of Cowley's letters might have preserved his name through those fluctuations of public taste which have so diminished his poetical reputation. To enjoy the reflective and familiar moods of Cowley we are now reduced to the "Essays," a slight collection, but often praised, with reason ; for theirs is a slowly distilled sweetness that grows more attractive by frequentation.

These essays are Epicurean in tone, an interesting fact revealed neither by Sprat's diffuse enthusiasm nor by Johnson's brief eulogy. Sprat does say that

104

COWLEY AND FRENCH EPICUREANS

Cowley intended them " as a real Character of his own thoughts, upon the point of his retirement," or, as we might say, a defence of his philosophy, which tended chiefly to place tranquillity of mind and indolence of body as the " sovereign good." Johnson merely notes of the "Essays": "His thoughts are natural, and his style has a smooth and placid equability which has never yet obtained its due commendation. Nothing is far-sought, or hard-laboured ; but all is easy without feebleness, and familiar without grossness." These discriminating criticisms (which make one wish that the plan of the " Lives " had permitted a more ample development) are technical, but Johnson's language shows he had perceived the philosophic tendency of the "Essays " ; naturalness and familiarity, " smooth and placid equability," are essentially Epicurean virtues. But Christians like Sprat and Johnson would not be likely to attribute any virtues to a philosopher so perverted from dogmatic gloom as to consider pleasure the object of life.

So few details of Cowley's life are preserved in Sprat's " funeral oration," and so scanty are other evidences from those disturbed times, that we know very little of Cowley's actions outside a few main points. We cannot tell exactly how he acquired his Epicureanism ; how far he practised it and with what results ; but the amiability, the delicacy in friendship, the love of solitude and obscurity in life which Sprat notes in him, are all definitely Epicurean. From the essays themselves we can learn with certainty what Cowley thought, and to them the reader is referred for confirmation or contradiction of these remarks.

When we say a man is an Epicurean, what do we mean ? Is it still necessary to say that " Epicurean " does not mean one who lives for selfish and sensual pleasures, a gourmet, a judge of vintages and cigars, a lifter of petticoats ? But even in its philosophic sense the term Epicurean is variously interpreted. Cowley's Epicureanism is intellectual and bourgeois, partly as a result of his temperament (for we are all born of one sect or another), and partly, this article wishes to suggest, as a result of his frequentation of Pierre Gassendi and his disciples. Undoubtedly, Cowley had read what was extant of Epicurus in his time (he quotes from him) and the " Life " in Diogenes Lærtius ; but Gassendi was most probably his master in philosophy.

We know from Sprat that Cowley was out of England from 1644 to 1656, part of the time in Paris, and though he was busily engaged as a royal secretary to the exiled English Court, it is hardly likely that Lord St. Albans kept him hard at work every day or that he had no access to Parisian society. We may surely assume that in twelve years Cowley made some acquaintances in France, and that some of these would be men of letters, and, when we find confirmation of it in his writings, we may still further assume that he was influenced by their conversation and culture—he wrote the "Davideis" at Cambridge, but the "Essays" when he returned from France.

Shorthouse has written a pleasant sketch of the English cavalier in Paris ; but all cavaliers were not, like Inglesant, visitors to Serenus de Cressy. Shorthouse assumes that the strong religious reaction, so powerful in the latter part of the reign of Louis XIV was dominant in French life between 1640 and 1660. There was such a movement under Louis XIII (the prosecution of Théophile de Viau in 1624 was its work), but at that King's death it languished ; regencies are seldom very moral. A glance at our Restoration drama shows that the exiled cavaliers were not greatly interested in religion, and indisputably our Restoration literature represents the influence of French culture and manners. Between 1645 and 1660 (which includes the Fronde) Epicureanism, scepticism, and libertinism were strong in French literary society ; the "Historiettes" of Tallemant show that they were not confined to men of letters. But the development and distinctions of French libertinism are so incorrectly represented by English critics that something more detailed and exact than usual may be welcome.

The father of the French libertins was Montaigne (not Epicurus), with a strong influence from Rabelais. The Epicureanism of Montaigne was a development of his own temperament. It differed from strict Epicureanism in many ways ; it was more Horatian and learned ; it relaxed that austere frugality of diet, it softened slightly the contempt for women (" The wise man shall not marry ") and failed in that civic respect for established religion which Epicurus enjoined. Hence French Epicureanism has always been more luxurious, more wanton, and more sceptical than a strict Epicurean would allow. In the seventeenth century Gassendi gave an immense impetus to Epicureanism by his lectures and books. His "De vita, moribus, et doctrina Epicuri " appeared in 1647 ; his notes on Diogenes Lærtius and the important "Syntagma" in 1649. He lectured at Paris from 1645 onwards. Now, when Gassendi and Epicurus were the topic of the day in cultured circles in Paris, is it likely that a natural Epicurean like Cowley would have failed to hear of them, and hearing of them, would fail to grow better acquainted with them ? Cowley certainly had heard of Gassendi, for he quotes him in the " Essays."

The intellectual Epicureanism of Gassendi was variously interpreted by his listeners and disciples. An acute but somewhat religious modern scholar, M. Frédèric Lachévre (whose admirable series of books on seventeenth-century libertinism is quite indispensable to a correct understanding of the movement), divides them into three distinct bodies : the *libertins avoués*, the *sceptiques*, and the *libertins politiques*. The *libertins avoués* were usually *goinfres* —that is, atheistical gluttons and whoremasters, who used the Epicurean doctrine as an excuse for their debauchery. Théophile de Viau was an early example of this sect (he was pre-Gassendi), while during Cowley's stay in Paris people like Des Barreaux Saint-Pavin, Blot, Cyrano de Bergerac, and Lignières kept up an enfeebled tradition of debauchery to the tune of—

> Ou je suis à la taverne,
> Ou j'y vais, ou j'en reviens.

The *sceptiques* were more respectable and attractive. They were by far the largest, most important, and varied group, and included at various times Molière and Dehénault, Chapelle and Gui Patin, Saint-Évremond and La Mothe Le Vayer. While they admitted more luxury than could have been allowed Metrodorus, for example, they represent the best of the movement, its most courtly and refined development. Finally, the then unimportant " *libertins politiques* " (philosophes born out of their due time) were represented by Cyrano, de Foigny, and Denis Vairasse d'Alais.

It should now be clear that to speak of the *libertins*

as one sect is injurious and incorrect. If, as we have imagined, Cowley was acquainted with the French Epicureans, he would certainly have been attracted by the more refined and courtly *sceptiques*. The crude debauchery of *libertins avoués* (represented in England by the works of writers like Wycherley and Rochester) would have been repulsive to his delicacy ; indeed, they were already discredited in France at that time, not so much by ferocious Church opposition as by a rapid softening of manners.

In the absence of any detailed proof we can only assume Cowley's intercourse with the *sceptiques*. Probably only a few scholars like M. Lachévre and M. Emile Magne are sufficiently acquainted with the life of the period to tell us who were Cowley's friends in Paris. But it may be claimed without undue exaggeration that Cowley found his natural tendencies greatly strengthened by the writings of Gassendi and his pupils. And, what is interesting, Cowley's Epicureanism is purer and more orthodox than that of most of the other Epicureans of the time. To parody a famous phrase, he was a naturally Epicurean soul. From childhood he loved solitude and study. Like Epicurus himself, he was not ardent towards women, and tradition definitely asserts the probability that the sentiments in "The Mistress" are feigned. He took away something of the austerity and simplicity of Epicureanism and substituted a fanciful

110

prettiness of his own invention; but even thus altered he was more orthodox than most of the Frenchmen—

A little convenient Estate, a little chearful House, a little Company, and a very little Feast, and if I were ever to fall in love again (which is a great Passion, and therefore I hope I have done with it) it would be, I think, with Prettiness rather than with Majestical Beauty.

He seems very near proclaiming himself a disciple of Epicurus in these lines—

When *Epicurus* to the World had taught,
    That pleasure was the chiefest good,
(And was perhaps i' th' right, if rightly understood)
    His life he to his Doctrine brought,
And in a Gardens shade that Sovereign Pleasure sought.

There is no need to remark on Cowley's intense love of flowers (so frequent in Greek and English poets) and of gardens. His essay " The Garden," addressed to Evelyn, begins with this truly Epicurean wish—

I never had any other desire so strong, and so like to Covet-ousness, as that one which I have had always that I might be master at last of a small House and large Garden, with very moderate Conveniencies joined to them, and there dedicate the remainder of my Life only to the Culture of them, and study of Nature. . . .

One might quote whole essays which are pure Epicureanism of a Latinized or Gallicized kind—not the clear Hellenic beauty recaptured by Landor. The very titles of his essays proclaim his doctrine —" Of Liberty," " Of Solitude," " The Garden," " The Dangers of an Honest Man in much Company." He quotes Montaigne, Gassendi, and Epicurus ; he translates many famous passages of Latin poetry which are Epicurean in tone, but chiefly from Horace. Seneca, Claudianus, Virgil, and Martial are represented, but not Lucretius, for Cowley's Epicureanism is more Horatian, pastoral, and elegiac than elevated and speculative. It is Church of England Epicureanism ; he keeps a gig in his stable. And yet sometimes he does teach that Epicurean charm which is so hard to define, as in that exquisite little Latin prayer which may be left in its original tongue since none will now wish to repeat it—

> Magne Deus, quod ad has vitæ brevis attinet horas,
> Da mihi, da Panem Libertatemque, nec ultra
> Sollicitas effundo preces : Si quid datur ultra
> Accipiam gratus ; sin non, contentus abibo.

Contentus abibo that is the correct note to end on ; for what is Epicureanism but contentedly minding one's own business in lettered solitude ?

X

MADAME DU DEFFAND AND
VOLTAIRE

MME. DU DEFFAND holds a distinguished place in French literature. She is one of that band of brilliant Frenchwomen whose achievements in literature give us reason to say that only the Greeks and the French have produced a body of really excellent work by feminine writers. The writings of the Greek poetesses have reached us only in poignant fragments ; we may gather them together piously and parsimoniously, they make but a slender volume, "all roses," it is true, but how few ; and we know so little about them. The barbarity of too many centuries of ignorance and turbulence interposes between us and the exquisite shadowy figures of old Greece ; we may speculate as we will, imagine life-stories, settings, tragedies for Anyte and Erinna and Nossis, "upon whose tablets Love melted the wax," but we shall never possess anything but a handful of doubtful dates, anecdotes, conjectures, and our own fancies. It is very different with these French women writers. So much is known and printed about them, they have been the objects of so many literary studies, that one's difficulty here is that of too great riches. In fact, with that human preference for what we have not over what we have, many of us no doubt would callously sacrifice a portion of our knowledge of the French ladies to know a little more about the Greeks. One would cheerfully exchange the works of Mme. Sand and Mme. Des Houlières, say, for Sappho and Corinna. But time and chance allow us no such bargains, and, failing the Greek women, we must make the best of the French. And within their own limits they have much to give us ; not, indeed, that Greek perfection which dissatisfies us for a time with everything else, but another more formal, less inspired, more worldly perfection of their own. In the writings of Mme. de La Fayette, Mme. de Sévigné, Mme. de Maintenon, Mme. du Deffand, there is a perfection of taste and wit, politeness, *usage du monde*, gaiety, *agrément*. They are the minor French classics, differing in degree from the Rochefoucaulds, the Bruyères, the Montesquieus, the Voltaires, but assuredly of their kind. They possess a polish, an ease, an impeccability, a complete freedom from all that is heavy, ridiculous, tedious, vapid, such as no Romantic writer, not even demi-classic Alfred de Vigny, can show. Put

down the letters of Mme. de Maintenon or Mme.
du Deffand and take up " Corinne " or a novel
of George Sand ; the difference is astonishing with
so short a period intervening. The guillotine and
the Code Napoléon had done their work well ; the
tyran and his minions were abolished, and with them
went for ever that distinction of living, thinking,
and feeling which made the French aristocracy
the arbiters of European manners and the dictators
of European culture.

In the long period of decline of that society
Mme. du Deffand holds a very important place :
" Elle est avec Voltaire, dans le prose, le classique
le plus pure de cette époque, sans même en excepter
aucun des grands écrivain." That is high praise
from a delicate critic like Sainte-Beuve, for Mme.
du Deffand's life covers the first eighty years of
the eighteenth century, a great period in French
literature ; to share the supremacy in that period
with Voltaire alone is to rank high indeed—above
Fontenelle, Montesquieu, Marivaux, d'Alembert, to
name four only. It is regrettable that the size of
this volume of selections from Mme. du Deffand's
letters forbade the inclusion of Voltaire's letters to
her as well as all hers to him. The comparison is
extremely interesting, and in any case a correspondence is a collaboration ; to give only one half of
the collaboration when the other half is extant

is disappointing. Moreover, no student of classic French can ever read too much Voltaire. Happily Voltaire's letters are all inserted in Lescure's " Correspondance Complète de la Marquise du Deffand," and in those two volumes the letters should be studied. To spend a week or more with these letters and then to turn abruptly to some modern novelist who is supposed to possess distinction is to experience a curious shock : this may not be the complete decadence that M. Anatole France believes it to be, but undoubtedly it is a change so immense that it is almost incredible. The French of Mme. du Deffand and Voltaire is practically a dead language.

The life and character of Mme. du Deffand have been studied and written so often that there is no information to add, and hardly any new critical deductions to be made. She was born in 1697, a year after the death of Mme. de Sévigné. She was educated at the Couvent de la Madeleine du Traisnel, Paris, one of those " couvents dévotes et galants " which have diverted the profane, scandalized the godly, and provided hundreds of true and false *contes* for generations. Marie de Vichy-Chamrond (as she was then) received there " une instruction sans principes et une éducation sans moralité," the source of many of her miseries and boredoms. While still a mere child she showed that tendency towards

116

scepticism which was so marked a trait in her
character. Massillon came to visit her, and was
charmed with her wit ; he advised that she should
read the Catechism. " J'étais comme Fontenelle,"
she says somewhere ; " j'avais à peine dix ans
que je commençais à n'y rien comprendre." More
than half a century later, when she was blind,
disappointed, and sick with the boredom of a dry
heart, she tried to recapture the " lost illusions
of religion." " Eh mais . . ." she interrupted the
person reading, " est-ce que vous comprenez quelque
chose à cela, vous ? " Women are sceptical and
irreligious, as they are mystic and religious, more
from temperament than conviction ; therefore they
tend to be more absolute in either than men. Mme.
du Deffand belonged to a not uncommon type—
the completely materialistic woman, whose metaphysical and religious senses are literally non-existent.
" Qu'est-ce que la foi ? " she writes Voltaire. " C'est
de croire fermement à ce qu'on ne comprend pas."
A different education might have crushed her wit,
saddened her youth, repressed her charm, and
turned her into a hypocrite ; but it could never
have given her another temperament.

Mlle. de Vichy became Mme. du Deffand in **1718**,
when the orgies of the Regency were at their height,
when the complete change of ancient traditions,
the *tohu-bohu universel* confused French society

profoundly ; when " le mariage, tel qu'il se pratique chez les grands est une indécence convenue." We hear of a brief *liaison* with the Regent, of Delrieu de Fargis, whispers of scandal from old memoirs ; and in 1722 Mme. du Deffand left her husband. For the next six years at least her life was that of all the expensive sensual pleasures, the gratification of egotism and vanity ; in 1728, at the age of thirty-two, she attempted a reconciliation with her husband, and the unhappy result was, to quote Mlle. Aïssé : " Elle reste la fable du public, blamée de tout le monde, méprisée de son amant, délaissée de ses amies."

At Sceaux, the Court of the Duchesse de Maine, Mme. du Deffand recovered that " consideration " she had temporarily lost and began her innocuous *liaison* with the Président Hénault. Her distinguished friends at that cultivated centre were numerous. In 1750 M. du Deffand died. In 1754 she went blind, and yet the most famous and enduring part of her life dates from that period. She had no amusement left but conversation, and her apartment in the convent of Saint Joseph became one of the most influential and delightful *salons* in Paris. The episode of Mlle. de Lespinasse and d'Alembert, and the curious passion of Mme. du Deffand for Horace Walpole alone disturbed the witty *ennui* of her days. After conversation, letters and books were her chief pleasure. Her letters place her high among French authors, though French literature is so rich in the genre. Her other art of conversation perished with her in 1780, but to touch even upon that circle of friends she delighted with her wit is impossible in an article. The reader must refer to the full and interesting pages of Lescure.

Before leaving the subject of Mme. du Deffand's life, something must be said of that perpetual *ennui* of which she constantly complained, that cold, depressing companion haunting the major part of her life. The *ennui* of Mme. du Deffand is famous and terrifying; one shrinks from the monotony of the everlasting *tædium vitæ* which nothing can atone for; not all her wit and reputation and exquisite tone could induce one to live a day of her life. She clung to Voltaire, partly because he was an old friend and she liked him, but partly because he helped to dissipate her *ennui*; the word recurs constantly in her letters to him—

Au nom de Dieu, tirez-moi de mon ennui . . .
. . . l'ennui qu'on ne peut éviter . . .
. . . je péris de langueur et d'ennui. . . .
Vous serez surpris, si je vous avoue que la perte de la vue n'est pas mon plus grand malheur; celui qui m'accable, c'est l'ennui.

In vain does M. de Voltaire exert himself to dissipate this eternal boredom of his friend, but the *ennui* which was the price of selfishness and " fashion " and elegant vices could not be charmed away by wit and sprightliness. Though she is obviously flattered by his attentions—she writes Walpole : " Je suis du dernier bien avec Voltaire ; j'ai reçu une lettre de lui de quatre pages aujourd'hui, en même temps que la vôtre ; il me comble d'amitiés et d'attentions "—flattery could not fill that terrible void of *ennui* approaching despair, any more than wit and delightful society. The natural and sober sentiments are very easily mocked at and easily discarded as useless, antique, and encumbering, yet they appear to be essential to happiness. Who but a person of more vanity than sense would exchange happiness for reputation or notoriety ? Mme. du Deffand sat in her *salon*, most envied, most quoted, most admired of exclusive hostesses ; but Julie de Lespinasse, the *confidante*, was holding her own *salon* in secret an hour before her patron's entrance, and Horace Walpole was in a perpetual cold perspiration of apprehension lest the old woman should make him ridiculous with her ill-placed passion. It was not the mere fact of becoming the Regent's mistress for a fortnight, not any of the scandals of her youth, which brought her to this pass where she was deceived by one friend and dodged by another ; it was the systematic stifling of all ordinary warm feelings under a naturally sceptical tempera-

ment, aided by fashionable cynicism. Mme. du
Deffand is always complaining to Voltaire of the
" cynicism and lack of taste " in the writers of the
day. Taste she possessed in perfection within her
narrow limits, but can we absolve of cynicism a
woman who repeats insistently—

. . . C'est qu'il n'y a, à le bien prendre, qu'un seul malheur
dans la vie, qui est celui d'être né. Il n'y a aucun état, quel
qu'il puisse être, qui me paraisse préférable au néant.

But, after all, we are not called upon to imitate
Mme. du Deffand's unskilful conduct of her life or to
share her (perhaps inevitable) *sécheresse de cœur* ;
we are to admire and to enjoy her wit and the purity
of her prose style. This very cynicism and hardness,
this incomprehension of all that we should call
Romanticism, make her an excellent critic of all
kinds of humbug. That eternal " ne pas être dupe "
of the French sceptics made her very quick to pierce
the weak point of pretentiousness. The solemn
flatness of society in that wig and gig period about
1760 is admirably summed up in a few caustic
words—

Il n'y a plus de gaieté, monsieur, il n'y a plus de grâces.
Les sots sont plats et froids, ils ne sont point absurdes ni
extravagants comme ils étaient autrefois. Les gens d'esprit
sont pédants, corrects, sententieux. Il n'y a plus de goût
non plus ; enfin il n'y a rien, les têtes son vides, et l'on veut
que les bourses le deviennent aussi. . . .

Naturally neither Diderot nor Rousseau, with their facile tears and their declamations and *attendrissements*, and their nature and virtue, could escape Mme. du Deffand's dislike. Even in these letters to Voltaire—but a fraction of the whole correspondence—we came across amusing little shafts at their expense—

. . . le jeu naturel que M. Diderot a prêché a produit le bon effet de faire jouer Agrippine avec le ton d'une harengère.

Of Jean-Jacques she writes—

C'est un plaisant ambition que de vouloir se rendre célèbre par les malheurs.

Voltaire's friends, the *philosophes* and the Encyclopédistes, found no mercy from her—

Je ne saurais admettre pour législateurs des gens qui n'ont que de l'esprit, peu de talent et point du goût. . . . On voit clairement qu'ils n'ont d'autre but que de courir après une célébrité on ils ne parviendront jamais.

Again—

Vos philosophes, ou plutôt soi-disant philosophes, sont de froids personnages : fastueux sans être riches, téméraires sans être braves, prêchant l'égalité par esprit de domination, se croyant les premiers hommes du monde, de penser ce que pensent tous les gens qui pensent ; orgueilleux, haineux, vindicatifs ; ils feraient haïr la philosophie.

The human comedy does not change much : the names of the various parts alter a little, the decorations are renewed, but the personages remain much the same. The *philosophes*, once *libertins*, transformed themselves into "fanatics" and "sectaries" in England; they have changed their names and invented a new kind of cant, that is all. No doubt they will create the same kind of mischief and misery their predecessors created, until such time as mankind learns a little common sense. And perhaps even now some cynical and bored old lady, with more wit than charity, is summing up the faults and follies of the age in casual letters destined to immortality. They will have to be very good to beat Mme. du Deffand's.[1]

[1] "Lettres à Voltaire." Par Madame du Deffand. Introduction de Joseph Trabucco. Paris, 1922.

XI

LETTERS OF MME. DE MAINTENON

THE extraordinary career of Mme. de Maintenon provides by itself a sufficient excuse for the numerous books of extracts and partial reprints of her letters, though, strangely enough, no complete edition has yet been issued. Mme. de Maintenon is entitled to a small but honourable and permanent place as a writer of French prose.

Interest in her as a writer is always in danger of disappearing in our greater interest in her enigmatic personality and singular destiny. To be born in a prison and die the widow of Louis XIV, to spend the early part of life in dependence, in poverty, and the latter part at Versailles ; to be granddaughter to the great Protestant leader Agrippa d'Aubigné and responsible in part for the Revocation of the Edict of Nantes—these antitheses of fortune are too piquant and romantic to escape the most careless attention. Perhaps it is but human to feel only curiosity about Mme. de Maintenon, not sympathy or affection for her memory. Or it may

124

be only perversity. But she is far too prudent and
virtuous and ultimately successful to be moving,
in spite of her romantic vicissitudes ; she is so much
the perfect governess and cultivated attendant—a
kind of Jane Eyre on a royal scale. She seems to
have been born to conduct youth, age, and infirmity
upon the paths of duty and reason, at no time of
her life, not even when she was only Mme. Scarron
or Françoise d'Aubigné, in the least yielding to
weaknesses, however amiable. The numerous scan-
dalous memorialists have been forced to spare
her name. Mme. de Maintenon herself says somewhere that her youth was happy and gay, she
described herself as " gay by nature and sad by
position " : but whatever her youth may have
been (and Sainte-Beuve, with something less than
his usual gallantry, says he would not put his hand
in the fire for her virtue) she appears to us now in
all the platitude of her thirty years' subjection to
her Royal husband. It is to no avail that we are
told of her youthful charm and wit, that she was
once a pretty girl, in fact ; she seems to have taken
on something of the imposing but wearisome grandeur
of Versailles ; she seems to have lost herself in
that terrible task of amusing a King who was " no
longer amusable," and as she says in a letter to
Mme. des Ursins, " perishing symmetrically " in
obedience to the Royal whim. The disasters of

125

the last years of the reign weighed heavily upon
them both—

Il est vrai, Madame [she writes to Mme. des Ursins, under
the date March 27, 1712], il est vrai, Madame, que je suis
triste : jamais personne n'a eu plus sujet de l'être ; mais
comptez que toute la cour l'est autant que moi. Tout manque,
tout paraît vide ; il n'y a plus de joie, plus d'occupation. Le
Roi fait tout ce qui lui est possible pour se consoler, et retombe
toujours dans ses premières douleurs ; il me les confie, et vous
sentez bien que c'est une grande augmentation à la mienne.

This intense grief was due less to the disasters of
France than to deaths in the Royal family. It was,
of course, natural that Louis XIV should feel deeply
the deaths of his brother, son, and grandson, and
that his wife should sympathize with him, but the
letters to Mme. des Ursins show very plainly that
singular overestimate of the Royal family which was
created by Louis's centralized power and naturally
appealed to the governess in Mme. de Maintenon.
The battles of Ramillies, Malplaquet, and Oudenarde
occupy less of Mme. de Maintenon's attention, are
written of in a less anxious tone, than the death
of the selfish, ignorant, and perverted Monsieur.
It was this Bourbonism in Mme. de Maintenon which
disgusted the Duc de Saint-Simon with her, in spite
of her profound piety and the services she had
rendered to Catholicism ; for the Duc was an ardent,
one might say a bigoted, Catholic. But the resigned
126

complacency of Mme. de Maintenon's religious sentiments could not weigh with Saint-Simon against
her efforts to secure the succession to the Throne
for Louis XIV's illegitimate children ; had an
archangel supported the Duc de Maine, Saint-Simon
would have hated him. Therefore the portrait
of Mme. de Maintenon drawn by the Duc, though
masterly from a literary point of view, is prejudiced
and unfair ; yet by exposing her essentially subaltern
feelings for the Royal family—which are rather
those of a favoured nurse than of a woman of penetration—Saint-Simon undoubtedly exposes one of
her least agreeable weaknesses. Sycophancy is too
harsh a word, but the weakness is in that direction.
It is not as if she had the excuse of a passion for
the King, which makes most people feel tenderly for
the memory of de la Vallière, for they were both
elderly when they married, and the King had no
affection left for anyone but his children ; indeed,
as M. Truc says of them, "they grew aged rather
than lived together." Simply from an excessive
domesticity Mme. de Maintenon thought that
twenty people in Versailles were more important
than all the rest of France. The sentiment might
be natural in the circumstances, but one cannot
admire it.

The two sets of letters in this volume cover
practically the whole of the reign of Louis XIV

from his majority to his death. The earlier period,
1660–93, is occupied by letters to her brother,
Charles d'Aubigné. It must always be admitted
to her credit that she barely changed her attitude
to her brother as her fortunes rose, and she was
extremely moderate in what she asked on his behalf ;
on the other hand, it must be remembered that her
power over the King was nothing compared with
that of Mme. de Montespan, whom he really loved,
and who destroyed her influence by her own incredible
folly. Even to her brother Mme. de Maintenon
plays the part of organizer and instructor, telling
him how to run his own house, how to manage his
own wife, how to reform his own existence—letters
of solemn exhortation which the mildest of modern
brothers would either put in the fire or answer with
a joke. The letter (No. X in this volume) dealing
with her sister-in-law is a perfect masterpiece of
family impertinence and interference. It was written
in 1678, when Mme. de Maintenon's position at
Court was fairly strong ; otherwise one cannot
imagine how d'Aubigné endured having his young
wife described as " une fille qu'on a gâtée," " d'une
incivilité insupportable," " de basse naissance,"
" déréglée en tout," " l'image de la bourgeoisie,"
" une caillette de Paris," and so on. She even
goes to the incredible extent of advising family
prayers and separate bedrooms.

The most important of the other letters in this first series are those written about the time of the Queen's death, when Mme. de Maintenon may have perceived the possibility of succeeding her. Yet, though she was in a sense an adventuress, she preserved always a real dignity and undertook her intrigues for the King's favour rather as a task on behalf of religion than as a means of gratifying ambition. Indeed, her position in the period between the Queen's death in 1683 and her own marriage to the King in 1685 seems to have filled her with misgiving and melancholy. She is obliged in one letter to combat d'Aubigné's accusations of depression ; it seems as if the sobriety, the sterility of her personality, so different from that of Mme. de Montespan, struck even her relatives. Her moderation in her unforeseen advancement is curious. In September 1684 she writes her brother—

Je ne pourrais vous faire connétable quand je le voudrais, et quand je le pourrais je ne le voudrais pas, étant incapable de vouloir rien demander de déraisonnable à celui à qui je dois tout, et que je n'ai pas voulu qu'il fît pour moi-même une chose au-dessus de moi.

The " thing above me " might have been a public marriage and recognition as Queen ; the words " incapable of wishing to ask for anything unreasonable " might almost stand as an epitaph to Mme. de Maintenon.

I

The letters to Mme. des Ursins are less intimate, more politic and political, more general, and, though historically more interesting, have a far slighter psychological value. " Mme. des Ursins " was the Princess Orsini, and had a political importance from her great influence in the Court of Spain. It was necessary, therefore, to conciliate and to exploit her. The passages which interest the modern reader are not so much the eternal " caquetage " about forgotten highnesses and extinct dukedoms, nor even the echo of political events, but the revelations of character in casual remarks or the occasional dramatic incident. There are certain phrases in all great collections of letters which suddenly bring us into actual contact with the past by a rapid firing of the imagination. The phrase " à l'heure que je vous écris, on joue *Esther* dans mon antichambre," or " M. d'Antin r .'a conté la morte de Mme. de Montespan," have this power of evocation, one hardly knows why. Such pleasures are perhaps factitious and non-existent for the majority of readers ; they are no doubt trivial. At the opposite extreme of dignity and importance is the restrained emotion of Mme. de Maintenon's letter on the death of the King—

Marly, le 11 Septembre, 1715.

Vous avez bien de la bonté, Madame, d'avoir pensé à moi dans le grand événement qui vient de se passer ; il n'y a qu'à baisser la tête sous la main qui nous a frappés.

130

LETTERS OF MME. DE MAINTENON

Je voudrais de tout mon cœur, Madame, que votre état fût aussi heureux que le mien. J'ai vu mourir le Roi comme un saint et comme un héros. J'ai quitté le monde que je n'aimais pas ; je suis dans le plus aimable retraite que je puisse désirer, et partout, Madame, je serai toute ma vie, avec le respect et l'attachement que je vous dois, votre très humble et très obéissante servante.

One may put that as an offset to Saint-Simon's odious misrepresentations of Mme. de Maintenon's conduct during the King's last illness. As everybody knows, Mme. de Maintenon left Versailles even before the King was dead and retired to Saint-Cyr with her memories. The last letter in the book gives us a strange last glimpse of Louis XIV's second wife, as she waited for the death she was persuaded would reunite them—

. . . j'ai quitté mes lunettes que j'avais prises il y a trente-cinq ans, et je travaille en tapisserie jour et nuit, car je dors peu ; ma retraite est paisible et très complète. Quant à la société, on ne peut en avoir avec des personnes qui n'ont nulle connaissance de ce que j'ai vu.

" Ce que j'ai vu " was the longest and in many ways the most important reign in French history. Mme. de Maintenon was connected with the Royal family of France for forty-five years, and for thirty years she was Louis's wife ; after all that immense effort and fatigue, that " comedy which begins every morning and ends only at night," it is chilling to

131

think of the sleepless and friendless old woman working night and day at her samplers. One might say of her life what a French critic said of Flaubert's masterpiece of disillusion : "Son goût du néant porte au cœur." [1]

[1] Mme. de Maintenon: "Lettres a D'Aubigné et Mme. des Ursins." Introduction de Gonzague Truc. Paris, 1923.

XII

THE PRINCE DE LIGNE

THE Prince de Ligne is an inexhaustible subject ; his Serene Highness—for the Lignes
are genuine Highnesses of the Empire—played
nearly as many parts in literature as in life. But,
like many royal and noble authors, the Prince suffered
from a plethora of experience and a famine of retirement ; all his books seem truncated by the necessity
of calling on the Emperor, setting out for Versailles,
or a new campaign or a new mistress ; they are
fragmentary and more remarkable for sudden sallies
of wit than the spirit of continuity. Thus we are
probably right in thinking the Prince more interesting than his books, the recital of what he did more
amusing at any rate than the record of what he
thought. When a man is as witty as the Prince
de Ligne there ought to be some means of making
him immortal for the benefit of posterity.

The " Mémoires " of the Prince de Ligne are fragmentary but extraordinarily interesting ; they seem
as if cut into paragraphs by his innumerable journeys,

for when he was still only middle-aged he calculated that he had spent 150,000 florins and three years of his life in travelling carriages. The Prince lived in the days when there was still a Europe and a European society, and he was a great traveller at a time when all journeys had to be made with horses. Before the year 1786, when the Turkish war and the subsequent revolutions in Belgium and France kept him in Vienna, he had made the journey from Brussels to Vienna, by way of Paris, thirty-four times, from the army to Vienna twelve times during three wars, from Beloeil to Paris eighteen times. It is not wonderful that his Mémoires are a little choppy.

The Prince's account of his childhood is the most vivid and curious part of this vivid, curious book. His father, Claude-Lamoral II de Ligne, was a singular character. He was a *grand seigneur* of the eighteenth century, when it was not the fashion to be a good husband or a good father. He did not love his son : " Je ne sais pas pourquoi," says the Prince, " car nous ne nous connaissions point." We are given a curious anecdote showing the old Prince's taste for ceremony and dignity : his wife was very much afraid of him, and was delivered of her child wearing a *grand vertugadin*, and died in the same costume a few weeks later. And yet the child was so carelessly baptized by the almoner of his father's regiment that his baptismal certificate could never be found. The old Prince thought himself a Louis XIV (and indeed his portrait shows something of the same well-nourished dignity), and squandered millions on his gardens and on magnificent display, giving entertainments worthy of a king. Yet he had bursts of ridiculous avarice, scolding his servants furiously for giving a glass of wine instead of beer to the chaplain who came to preach in Lent. His idea of education was curious : he gave his son a variety of tutors, most of them ignorant, but never any money. The young Prince was allowed a small sum of money for each head of game he brought in, but had to buy his own powder and shot, and never had any money but what he earned in this way until he was married. The result of his changing tutors was a certain religious confusion ; the young Prince was at one time of his childhood a Molinist, then a Jansenist, and then an atheist ; when it came to the time for his first Communion it was discovered he knew nothing about Christianity, and he had to be instructed by the village priest, "qui n'y comprenait rein non plus que moi." Add to this remarkable education the fact that the usual attentions he received from his father were gloomy prognostics of his future, and remarks that he would be "un sujet détestable," and it is not hard to understand the peculiar nonchalance in matters of religion and family affection so characteristic of the eighteenth-century *seigneur*.

The marriage of the young Prince was conducted in the same off-hand way. Without a word of explanation, the father took his son in his carriage to Vienna and introduced him to a household where there were " quantité de jolies figures épousées ou à épouser." The Prince learned from his servants that he was to marry one of them, dined with them without the least idea which of them was proposed for him, and was married a week later. The Prince was eighteen, his wife fifteen ; they had never spoken to each other, and therefore it is not surprising that he treated the matter as " bouffon " for the first few weeks, and then as " indifférent." " Now if this were represented upon the stage it would be condemned as an improbable fiction," as bad dramatists used to make a character say to excuse some more than ordinary improbability ; but in this case the whole thing, though improbable, is quite true. And the joking tone in which the Prince relates it fails to conceal, even at this distance of time, the wounding of his feelings by this amazingly high-handed treatment. Yet the Prince respected his father extremely, and was probably more moved at his death than the members of the generations whose childhood was lavishly spoiled and who repaid

it by an extravagant abuse. The seigneurial disregard of others' feelings displayed by the Prince
Claude-Lamoral II is outrageous but impressive;
the instinct that mere domesticity and the sentimental feelings generally ought to be subjected
to one's duty (to the King, one's caste, one's family)
is not a despicable one, even though some may think
it was carried to an excess in this case.

The Prince de Ligne readily adopted the eighteenth-
century cynicism of his class—

> Je ne me souviens plus si ce fut par air ou par goût pour la
> chasse que j'y allai à six heures du matin après la première
> nuit de mes noces. Il est vrai que ma belle-mère nous était
> venue réveiller avant le jour, de peur, disait-elle, que de
> mauvaises gens ne nous jetassent un sort. Je m'aperçus bien
> que la famille dans laquelle j'étais entré n'était pas grande
> sorcière.

The Prince is as witty and careless about his
marriage as the hero of a comedy by Regnard;
we can only comment on his wit, as the valet usually
does in such comedies, with the exclamation
" Peste ! " It is almost indecent for a man to be
so persistently witty. One day when the Prince
was late for dinner with the King of Poland, he
excused himself as follows—

> Sire, c'est une de vos plus belles sujettes qui en est la cause.
> Son secret sera bien gardé, car il m'est impossible de me
> ressouvenir de son nom, qui est de cinq ou six syllabes
> diaboliques à prononcer.

Nobody had more "cheek"—we should call it now—than the Prince de Ligne in his dealings with royalty. Only Marie Antoinette was spared his worst shafts, and even with her he took liberties. The Queen was once at a ball given by a lady whose lover was an officer in the Guards; the Queen desired that the orchestra should play a lively air, and Ligne at once suggested, to the utter confusion of the hostess, that they should play a song beginning—

> Dans les gardes françaises,
> J'avais un amoureux.

His remark to Mme. du Barry was cutting. One morning in the King's presence, at her toilette, she asked the Prince for a note of some affair ; he replied that he had given it to her coiffeur to make into curl papers because "c'était le seul moyen de lui mettre une affaire dans la tête." Louis XV was enchanted, and went about repeating the joke. And yet one of the Prince's lamentations in life was that people did not always see his jokes, and he relates the following anecdote in proof of it. The Archduke Albert had been defeated at the battle of Jemappes ; a little while after he asked the Prince de Ligne if he (the Archduke) were much changed by an illness he had recently had. "Monseigneur," said Ligne, "je vous trouve l'air encore un peu *défait*." The Archduke failed to see the

138

jest. Only on one occasion did the Prince completely lose his presence of mind, and that was from a guilty conscience. He and the Emperor were in love with the same lady, and, unknown to the Emperor, Ligne was sharing the lady's favours. One night at the opera the Emperor unexpectedly came into the box where they were, throwing them into a state of nervousness which drove Ligne stammering from the box when the Emperor innocently asked the title of the play : it was Lesage's "Crispin rival de son Maître."

All this brilliance at the Courts of Vienna, St. Petersburg, and Versailles was not achieved without some expense. The Prince lost his vast estates in Belgium when the Revolutionary and Napoleonic armies advanced eastward. He calculated that he had spent 500,000 florins on his campaigns and given 200,000 to the various troops he had commanded ; 500,000 in building, gardens, entertainments ; his " house " in Belgium 60,000 florins, his " maison ambulante " 40,000 florins, and so on. He calculated he had spent about 20,000,000 francs, but this is an underestimate, says his editor, M. Leuridant. Even after the triumph of Napoleon he contrived to live in a certain amount of state and luxury, giving dinners to sixty or more people every week.

There is one point in these " Mémoires " worth stress-

ing, and that is the Prince's chivalrous and sincere
defence of Marie Antoinette. He confesses that he
had once been half in love with her—as apparently
everyone was—but denies strenuously the many
odious calumnies against her. The Prince de Ligne
was the Queen's intimate for six years; he not
only disproves the usual calumnies against the
Queen, but shows how one of the vilest of all was a
misrepresentation of an act and an emotion which
was not only perfectly innocent, but touching and
highly creditable. Yet even the tragedies of the
Revolution and the destruction of his world did not
quench the old man's wit and sparkle. He survived
until the Congress of Vienna (raging that the Austrians
would not give him an army to measure himself
against Napoleon), and his comment on that august
meeting is familiar to all the world—" Le Congrès
danse mais ne marche pas." The last entry in his
" Mémoires " runs : " Le Congrès est à bout de fêtes :
quel spectacle lui donnerai-je pour le désennuyer ?
l'enterrement d'un maréchal." A few days later
he died ; let us hope the Congress was suitably
amused.

XIII

LANDOR'S " HELLENICS "

FEW books of great poetry are so difficult to appraise justly as the "Hellenics." To state the difficulties may remove some preliminary obstacles to the enjoyment of a kind of poetry so rare in English that no obvious analogues suggest themselves.

To-day no writer whose books survive can be called forgotten ; and in no sense are the " Hellenics " forgotten. Perhaps they are neglected and perhaps they are underestimated by that " general reader " of poetry who is much more important than the literary " Fossores " who exhume obscure and forgotten writers in their antiquarian zeal or bind on their brows a barren garland of praise for some wholly unnecessary researches. The comparative neglect of the "Hellenics"—compared, that is, with the writings of popular poets like Shelley and Tennyson—would not perhaps deter this hypothetical reader, though the scarcity of the book might cause him to miss it. There are other obstacles. First,

141

Landor's poetry is not a favourite with the literary essayists who are supposed to influence public taste. Then the most distinguished admirer of Landor happened to be Swinburne, whose verbose and almost frantic adulation is more likely to lose than to gain sympathy; while other more persuasive critics with greater restraint if less genius and intuition simply and baldly rank Landor as second-rate. Again, the anthologies—which we are told supply the general reader with specimens upon which he forms his preliminary judgment—represent Landor almost exclusively by his epigrams. Except "Artemidora," no poem from the "Hellenics" is generally quoted. And then it is the general opinion, which seems to be the correct one, that Landor's prose is more important than his poetry. Besides all this, some potential readers are certainly deterred by the somewhat foolish popular anecdotes (like the story about throwing the man out the window) and still more by the portrait of Boythorn in "Bleak House," which is generally held to represent Landor. Boythorn is not unamiable, but he is ridiculous, and people do not like poets to be too ridiculous. Boythorn may be a true portrait of Landor's exterior and yet be false to his genius for, though Dickens had an incomparable gift in observing oddities of behaviour, he was a Philistine in matters of taste.

These are some of the reasons why Landor's

poetry is seldom mentioned in comparison with that of his more famous contemporaries, Coleridge, Byron, Wordsworth, Blake, Keats, Scott, Shelley. He is often ranked with Rogers and Campbell—a little below Tom Moore, if a little above Hemans. Like his friend, Southey, he is often little more than a name as a poet. Of course there is no exact method of discovering how much the "Hellenics" are read and admired ; Landor may be intensely appreciated by a large, silent audience, but he is certainly not fashionable, and probably never will be. The true cause of this comparative obscurity is not so much the little accidents enumerated, but Landor's poetic style itself, the ideal of poetry he deliberately set himself, in opposition to the tendencies of eighteenth-century moralizing poetry and nineteenth-century decorative poetry. In the preface to the "Hellenics," written with that brusque terseness he affected towards the public, he says : "Little in these pages will gratify the generality of readers. Poetry, in our day, is oftner prismatic than diaphanous : this is not so : they who look into it may see through." The phrase "oftner prismatic than diaphanous"—a fine terse criticism of the Romantic movement—gives a first clue to a correct appreciation of Landor's poems. The poetry of the great Romantics and their successors is so often merely "prismatic" ; deficient in architectural quali-

ties but abounding in picturesque details and irri-
descent language. Matthew Arnold's criticism of
" Isabella " marks a cardinal weakness of Romantic
poetry, from which the critic himself was by no
means free when he wrote poetry. Now the style
of Landor is deliberately architectural and " classic,"
perhaps the most classic (in intention) of all our poets ;
Landor is the most determined to reproduce in
English the effects of earlier Greek poetry, the most
consistent in his poetical ideal and the most ruthless
expunger of every tendency and influence foreign
to his ideal. Most people will admit that Arnold
had a lofty ideal of the poetic art, and that he also
attempted to make English some of the " classic "
qualities of Greek poetry. A comparison is
interesting.

> Far, far from here
> The Adriatic breaks in a warm bay
> Among the green Illyrian hills ; and there
> The sunshine in the happy glens is fair,
> And by the sea, and in the brakse.
> The grass is cool, the sea-side air
> Buoyant and fresh, the mountain flowers
> As virginal and sweet as ours.

That is " prismatic " poetry. Now turn from
that romantic nostalgia to the " diaphanous " lines
which open Landor's poem " To Corinth "—

> Queen of the double sea, beloved of him
> Who shakes the world's foundations, thou hast seen
> Glory in all her beauty, all her forms ;

Seen her walk back with Theseus when he left
The bones of Sciron bleaching to the wind,
Above the ocean's roar and cormorant's flight,
So high that vastest billows from above
Show but like herbage waving in the mead ;
Seen generations throng the Isthmian games,
And pass away ; . . .

Note Arnold's weak adjectives : " warm, green, happy, fair, cool, buoyant, fresh, virginal, sweet " —so many of them " literary " and unnecessary ; and then look at Landor's : " double, high, vastest, Isthmian." Does not that mark the difference between a weak, emotional poet and a strong " classic " poet. And if we are compelled to say that of Arnold's poetry, how much more of Swinburne's !

To use the word " classic " in describing a style is to invite misapprehension and dissent. And yet " Hellenic " alone does not define the quality of Landor's poetry at its best. He is the most deliberately Hellenic of English poets ; even his quaint-sounding laconisms are an attempt to achieve Greek brevity. But however Greek his mind and tastes, Landor himself was a choleric English gentleman with tremendous pride, a manner at once violent and courteous, blustering and dignified, and above all, a heart of the most tender delicacy and generosity ; and this English character is continually invading his Hellenism, even in the most objective of his

K   145 poems. If Dickens had made the canary Lesbia's sparrow he might have given the portrait of Boythorn a sort of mythopæic sense : one sees the British barbarian subjugated by the Attic muse. The peculiar circumstances of Landor's life and temperament easily allowed him to imagine himself now as Pericles, now as Epicurus, now as Sophocles, now as Diogenes. He lived so familiarly with great men that proud speech came naturally to him. But his charming tenderness for women is chivalric and quite unhellenic, even though he may have persuaded himself that sentiment as delicate as his existed in the ancient world. Landor's Hellenism has a double aspect : it comes chiefly from his affinity with the spirit of Greek thought, from his understanding of the Greek ideal, from his possessing a " Greek soul "—as we say sentimentally ; but it comes also from an instinctive checking of his English emotionalism. He lived in a series of emotional explosions ; of wrath, pride, generosity, tenderness, indignation. How natural that he should turn for discipline to the pure serenity of Attic Greek ; and knowing him as we do, how natural that Walter Savage Landor, fuming with rage over some trifle, should invest his indignation (at some local squire) with the Jovian dignity of Pericles or the cynic indifference of Diogenes. The English Landor is always visible through the Greek Landor, even in

146

the " Hellenics" ; the matter, the form, almost the
very speech is Greek, but the voice is English. One
suspects that his chaste Hellenic maidens wore
corkscrew curls ; certainly his Agamemnons and
Ptolemys, Hyperbions and Rhaicos have all been
christened " Walter Savage " while the republican,
or rather oligarchic, sentiment is too violent, the
generosity too open and quixotic to fit a nation
of genial liars and unscrupulous intriguers like the
Athenians. Moreover, Landor's culture, though
primarily, was not exclusively Hellenic. He was
very extensively read in Latin, with an exceptionally
wide knowledge of neo-Latin authors ; he was
nourished on the best in the literatures of Italy,
France, and England. And he was one of our great
critics. If he was not learned in any cumbersome
or pejorative sense, he possessed a culture as choice
and as enthusiastic as that of Goethe, if not so
extensive. The matter of Landor's affinity with
the great classical school of Germany (now absurdly
disparaged) must be left to those more competent.
I am not sufficiently acquainted with German to
attempt it. Yet there is a little anecdote of Goethe
which is suggestive. It is said that when Goethe
had been disturbed by emotional or tedious visitors,
he regained his calm by looking at his Greek marbles ;
in the same way Landor recovered his serene dignity
in the company of Homer and Sophocles.

It would be impossible for Landor's style to be purely Hellenic—he would have had to be born Greek for that—and so the much-abused " classic " still seems the correct work. After all, " classic " implies many of the qualities Landor most admired ; and it implies also the opposite of all " prismatic " and all turgidly unplastic poetry. But the Greeks were Landor's masters. Unlike Keats, he did not get his Hellenism at second hand through the kaleidoscope of Jacobean English poetry. Landor says somewhere that he was brought up on Greek and Latin poetry, and that when he began to read English poets they all seemed tame and undignified except Milton. Yet, though he paid Milton that tremendous compliment, he was too haughty or too much of an artist to use Milton's style. Perhaps a nice discrimination could detect Milton's influence in the " Hellenics," but in general their style is modelled on the sententious brevity of poets like Simonides, with a certain alloy of Latinisms. Notice in the following lines the rather excessive attempt at Greek simplicity and brevity—

> The sea shines bright before us. What white sail
> Plays yonder ? What pursues it ? Like two hawks
> Away they fly. Let us away in time
> To overtake them. Are they menaces
> We hear ? And shall the strong repulse the weak
> Enraged at her defender ? Hippias !
> Art thou the man ? 'Twas Hippias. He had found

His sister borne from the Cecropian port
By Thrasymedes.   And reluctantly ?
Ask, ask the maiden ; I have no reply.

Imagine that passage re-written in the "prismatic" style of Shelley ; it would occupy at least
a page.   Observe that this is not the Gallic classicism
of Pope nor the moralized and over-formal classicism
of Johnson nor verbalized Hellenism like that of
"Balaustion's Adventure" ; it represents an almost
unique and not very successful attempt to force
into English classic density and terseness.   The
result is sometimes more strange than beautiful,
for, to achieve it, Landor boggles at no obscurity,
no allusiveness, no awkward Latinism.   The mere
reconditeness of his allusions is sufficient to daunt
some readers who will need the classical dictionary
nearly as much for the "Hellenics" as for the Meta-
morphoses.   A timid reader is not encouraged by
lines like these—

The proud Æmonian shook Aëtion's towers.
Alpheios and Spercheios heard the shout
Of Mænalos ; Cyllenè, Pholoë,
Parthenos, Tegea, and Lycaios, called. . . .

These, if not defects in an English poem, can
hardly be called beauties ; still less the frequent
Latinisms, like "*illuded* into love," "with light
he *irrigates* the earth," "*pubescent* flower," "*lustral*
water" and "*radiant* nod."   The search for brevity

and simplicity, the avoidance of the " prismatic " lead to some queer banalities when (as rarely happens) Landor loses his dignity—

> Thou hadst *evinced the madness of thy passion* . . .
> Whatever is most *laudable and manly* . . .
> *Flapping* the while with laurel-rose
> The honey-gathering tribes away. . . .

Yet when all these difficulties and defects have been recorded, when we add to them the peculiar spelling Landor affected and the occasional lack of spontaneity in the language (due perhaps to some of the poems having been written in Latin and then translated into English), then we have simply cleared away the obstacles which prevent enjoyment of the poetry of the "Hellenics." When the reader perceives Landor's ideals and method, the difficulties begin to vanish, the defects become insignificant. Those whose taste is chiefly formed on romantic poetry, those who are entirely seduced by modern impressionism, will probably not enjoy the "Hellenics." You cannot find witty or pointed couplets or lovely suave phrases (so abundant in Keats and Tennyson) nor any of the coloured fumes of mysticism in Landor's poetry. Landor is never verbose. Harsh, over rapid, too condensed, too allusive, too " diaphanous," perhaps ; but never dull, never diffuse, never ignoble, never turgid and vague.

LANDOR'S " HELLENICS "

Because the poet worked for the architectural qualities of poetry, the "Hellenics" are not easily quotable. Landor's unit is not the line, not the passage, but the poem. To quote fragments of the "Hellenics" is to show a limb or a torso instead of the whole statue. And even so it is not hard to discover lovely things in the "Hellenics." Here is a well-known stanza in Landor's rarer lyric strain—

> Tanagra ! think not I forget
>   Thy beautifully-storied streets ;
> Be sure my memory bathes yet
>   In clear Thermodon, and yet greets
> The blithe and liberal shepherd-boy,
> Whose sunny bosom swells with joy,
> When we accept his matted rushes
> Upheaved with sylvan fruit ; away he bounds and blushes.

The last line is not quite so felicitous as one would wish, and appears as if it had troubled the poet throughout, yet felicity is never lacking in the epigrams, so we must conclude the disappointing movement is deliberate. Landor's poetic genius was not lyric ; it lay rather in dialogue and narrative. English taste insists that all poetry shall sing ; without reflecting that nobody would sing a narrative. But because Landor did not sacrifice everything to sound and " prismatic " conceits it does not follow that he is lacking in richness. When for a while he relaxes from his Attic severity into a more Sicilian mood, few poets are capable of such richness—

> In spring we garland him with pointed flowers,
> Anemone and crocus and jonquil,
> And tender hyacinth in clustering curls ;
> Then with sweet-breathing mountain strawberry ;
> Then pear and apple blossom, promising
> (If he is good) to bring the fruit full-ripe,
> Hanging it round about his brow, his nose,
> Down even to his lips.   When autumn comes,
> His russet vine-wreath crackles under grapes :
> Some trim his neck with barley, wheat, and oat ;
> Some twine his naked waist with them ; and last
> His reverend head is seen and worshipped through
> Stiff narrow olive-leaves, that last till spring.

" Pointed flowers," " sweet-breathing mountain strawberry," " stiff narrow olive-leaves "—are not such phrases the very marrow of Theocritus ? Is it only a romantic fancy which makes one feel that no poets were ever so sensitive to the crisp outlines and clear tints of flowers and fruits as the Greeks ? Landor shared that exquisite plastic feeling. Only a poet who is so gifted with the love and understanding of their beauty can so evoke their essential form and colour and scent. The demi-gods whom the Greek poets invented as the spirits of flowers and trees and windy rocks were a projection of this sensitiveness. And Landor, the tender old Englishman, understood so well that delicate

respect for beauty. His Hamadryad says to
Rhaicos—

> And wouldst thou too shed the most innocent
> Of blood ? no vow demands it ; no God wills
> The oak to bleed.

And again—

> I have no flock : I kill
> Nothing that breathes, that stirs, that feels the air,
> The sun, the dew. Why should the beautiful
> (And thou art beautiful) disturb the source
> Whence springs all beauty ? Hast thou never heard
> Of Hamadryads ?

There is nothing mawkish in this sentiment. The
idylls which compose the "Hellenics" are chiefly
heroic. Landor can express the finest emotions of
the lover of beauty and understand wild flowers
like a sensitive woman ; but he can also express
fortitude with vehement eloquence. There is no
weak pathos in his dying Achilles—

> Not that Larissa in a quiet tomb
> Holds my brave ancestors grieve I, O Death,
> Not that my mother will lament my loss,
> Lone in the bower of Tethys, for a while ;
> I grieve that Troy should ever thus exult
> Without more slaughter of the faithless race.
> Open the turf, removed the blackened boughs,
> And let the urn of Menætiades
> Take my bones too.

Landor's dramatic conceptions, sometimes a little
strained, are nearly always heroic and dignified.

He has imagined a great emotional situation in the meeting of the shades of Agamemnon and Iphigeneia, when she—not knowing he has been murdered by her mother—exclaims at his turning back his head in shame—

> Beloved father ! is the blade
> Again to pierce my bosom ? 'tis unfit
> For sacrifice ; no blood is in its veins ;
> No God requires it here ; here are no wrongs
> To vindicate, no realms to overthrow.
> You are standing as at Aulis in the fane,
> With face averted, holding (as before)
> My hand ; but yours burns not, as then it burn'd ;
> This alone shows that we are with the Blest,
> Nor subject to the sufferings we have borne.
> I will win back past kindness.
>   Tell me then,
> Tell how my mother fares who loved me so,
> And griev'd as 'twere for you, to see me part.
> Frown not, but pardon me for tarrying
> Amid too idle words, now asking how
> She prais'd us both (which most ?) for what we did.

It is hardly possible that the "Hellenics" could become popular. Many, whose taste is formed on less august models, will never feel the pure heroic beauty of the "Hellenics." Yet Landor will always find some enthusiasts to prefer the " diaphanous " beauties of the "Hellenics" to the more dazzling but less satisfying attractions of " prismatic " poetry.

XIV

VICTOR HUGO AND "LA LÉGENDE DES SIÈCLES"

"LA LÉGENDE DES SIÈCLES" was designed by its author as an Epic of Progress. It was published in 1859, so that only sixty years elapsed between its first appearance and its inclusion in the series of "Grands Écrivains de la France," which is a kind of final homage to the illustrious. Yet, if one may judge from the date at the end of M. Paul Berret's excellent introduction, this edition would have appeared in 1914 had the publication not been delayed by a grand expression of Progress. A curious coincidence that this magniloquent praise of Progress should have been delayed six years by a European war; that this homage should be paid it at the very moment when its main idea is heavily discredited.

Hugo's faith in mechanically propelled vehicles as an evidence of Progress (the capital "P" seems as appropriate as in the allied Podsnappery), as a proof of civilization, even as being civilization itself, is

childish and commonplace, though he was not the
only one to mistake the husk for the kernel, the
science of mechanics for the art of life. His Satyr
prophesies railways in these words—

> Qui sait si quelque jour on ne te verra pas,
> Fier, suprême, atteler les forces de l'abîme,
> Et, dérobant l'éclair à l'Inconnu sublime,
> Lier ce char d'un autre à des chevaux à toi ?

He describes the *Great Eastern* steamship as—

> . . . un monstre à qui l'eau sans bornes fut promise,
> Et qui longtemps, Babel des mers, eut Londres entier
> Levant les yeux dans l'ombre au pied de son chantier,
> Effroyable, à sept mâts mêlant cinq cheminées
> Qui hennissaient au choc des vagues effrénées.

And his description of an aeronaut as a " fier
cocher Du char aérien que l'éther voit marcher " is
even more amusing. Fier cocher ! And he seems
to have thought a dirigible could fly to Sirius and
back—

> Ciel ! ainsi, comme on voit aux voûtes des celliers
> Les noirceurs qu'en rôdant tracent les chandeliers,
>   On pourrait, sous les bleus pilastres,
> Deviner qu'un enfant de la terre a passé,
> A ce que le flambeau de l'homme aurait laissé
>   De fumeé au plafond des astres !

Yet, even though the naïveté of Hugo's faith in
machines is ridiculous, though his Progress is now a
demolished illusion, is his epic necessarily valueless ?

"*LA LÉGENDE DES SIÈCLES*"

We do not believe in Homer's gods or Dante's theology, yet we do not deny that the Iliad and the Commedia are great poems. Lucretius made a great poem out of philosophic doubt, Dante out of religious belief; but it is not necessary to agree with either to appreciate his poem. In fact, when we find any person who does not admire both the " De rerum Natura " and the " Commedia Divina " we know that such a one is defective in taste and sensibility. We do not go to poetry for science. All Hugo's unfortunate cumber of balloons and railways and *Great Eastern* steamers is only worse than Milton's cannons and bridge over chaos because they are made a more important part of his work by the Frenchman. In reading "La Légende des Siècles" we must not be worried by accessories to which the author gave a disproportionate attention; we must not even trouble about the truth or falsity of his main theme. We must look for other qualities and other excellences.

What was fine in Hugo was his love of human beings, his persuasion that on the whole men are more good than bad, his hatred of oppression, meanness, cruelty, and greed, his humanity and sympathy, his gifts as an imaginative writer. You may show that his Progress was principally the popular self-deception of the last century, that he was melodramatic, a wind-bag, that he humbugged himself, that

157

he plagiarised shamefully, that his erudition was a sham and his local details a mere collection of bric-à-brac ; and when all that is said and proved it has not destroyed Victor Hugo, it has not contaminated the essence of his poetry. You cannot dispose of passages like the following by simply calling them rhetorical—

Oh ! les lugubres nuits ! Combats dans la bruine !
La nuée attaquant, farouche, la ruine !
Un ruissellement vaste, affreux, torrentiel,
Descend des profondeurs furieuses du ciel ;
Le burg brave la nue ; on entend les gorgones
Aboyer aux huit coins de ses tours octogones ;
Tous les monstres sculptés sur l'édifice épars,
Grondent, et les lions de pierre des remparts
Mordent la brume, l'air et l'onde, et les tarrasques
Battent de l'aile au souffle horrible des bourrasques ;
L'âpre averse en fuyant vomit sur les griffons ;
Et sous la pluie entrant par les trous des plafonds,
Les guivres, les dragons, les méduses, les drées,
Grincent des dents au fond des chambres effondrées. . . .

Nor is it a complete criticism to say that " Les Pauvres Gens " and similar poems are sentimental. There is something real in lines like these—

La mère, se sentant mourir, leur avait mis
Sa mante sur les pieds et sur le corps sa robe,
Afin que, dans cette ombre où la mort nous dérobe,
Ils ne sentissent plus la tiédeur qui décroit,
Et pour qu'ils eussent chaud pendant qu'elle aurait froid.

Add to these the portrait of Philip II of Spain in " La Rose et l'Infante," the parricide's spirit under

the rain of blood, the scene in the great hall in
" Eviradnus," the lugubrious warnings of the ten
sphinxes, the dramatic lines in " Le Petit Roi de
Galicie," when

> Le chevalier leva lentement sa visière :
> Je m'appelle Roland, pair de France, dit-il . . .

and they still are only part of the fine things
scattered through the pages of " La Légende des
Siècles."

After reading these passages most people who are
not affected with excessive modernity will agree that
Hugo was a poet.　But if we are to keep a just sense
of proportion we cannot compare him with the
greater poets already mentioned.　Still less can we
speak of him as French enthusiasts, who think he is
like Shakespeare but rather better.　" La Légende
des Siècles " is not an epic at all ; it is a collection
of dramatic and narrative poems.　If they are to be
compared with anything it is with " Men and
Women " and " Poems and Ballads."　And Hugo
is not always up to that standard.　Too often he
strikes an English reader as an inferior Browning
writing in the style of an inferior Swinburne.　He is
less subtle than the author of " In a Balcony " ; and
he never wrote anything so sustained, so eloquent, and
so harmonious as " Atalanta in Calydon."　Modesty
and self-depreciation were not characteristics of

Hugo ; the kind of poem Browning was content to call a dramatic lyric Hugo called an epic. He had a mania for the grand and sublime, which too often with him meant the grandiose and the rhetorical. He tried to match himself with Shakespeare, but his best is not equal to Shakespeare's second best. He caught from Chateaubriand tricks of eloquence and phrase-making which do not always lead to complete sincerity. After Hugo, it is small wonder we had M. Jules Romains asking for poetry to be " nu et sobre." Hugo adopted the attitude of a prophet, of an inspired guider of weak humanity, a most difficult part to sustain before an enlightened public. Modern curiosity is too unscrupulous, criticism too searching, means of information too common for any man to be able to pose so grandly with success. We know too much about Hugo to be able to take him at his own estimate.

It makes no difference to one's estimate of Hugo's genius to learn that he collected much of his information from Moréri's dictionary, that he used that information carelessly, that his poems are full of blunders, anachronisms, sonorous names which mean nothing. One does not even object to his numerous plagiarisms from less-known contemporaries. But he cannot be exonerated when he is cheap or silly or a dupe, for such defects seriously mar his work. There is no doubt that Hugo was deceived by table-rappings.

" *LA LÉGENDE DES SIÈCLES* "

The spirits of Molière, Shakespeare, Dante, Æschylus, a toad, the lion of Androcles, the Angel of Light, all dictated poems (written in French) in the style of Victor Hugo, containing the ideas in which he was then interested. He seems never to have regarded these manifestations with anything but credulous awe ; never to have suspected that they might be a subconscious thought transference through that " marvellous medium," Charles Hugo. The influences of these séances may be traced in " Le Satyre " and particularly in " Plein Ciel " and " Plein Mer." The pontifical and raving manner so displeasing in Hugo came from the fact that he regarded himself as inspired by God. M. Louis Barthou possesses a photograph of Hugo in an ecstatic pose with half-shut eyes, inscribed in the poet's handwriting : " V. Hugo écoutant Dieu."

If Hugo was a dupe in such matters, he was cheap in his snarlings at Napoleon III. It is the privilege of poets and prophets to denounce kings and governments, but not from motives of disappointed ambition. M. Berret tries to excuse Hugo by saying he was " always a liberal " ; but why did he wait until he had been several times passed over for Cabinet rank before he found it out ? Like Chateaubriand before him, he was corroded by disappointed political ambitions. " That is the speech of a man who has tried vainly for thirty years to enter the Cabinet,"

L

said Montalembert after hearing the famous denunciation of Napoléon le Petit. Unhappily, Montalembert was right. Who now can avoid a feeling of irritation at these furious denunciations of wounded vanity masquerading as an altruistic passion for the public welfare ?

> Oh ! pourquoi la souffrance et pourquoi la laideur ?
> Hélas ! le bas-empire est couvert d'Augustules,
> Les Césars de forfaits, les crapauds de pustules. . . .

Excellent invective, but how much more convincing if the author had not first vainly tried for a portfolio from Augustule.

Even Hugo's humanitarianism was a little silly. M. Berret tells an anecdote of a dinner scene. The Master says : " I saved a lizard to-day." Someone else says : " I saved a spider " ; someone else : " I saved a crab." Then everyone tells in turn how he did it, and the Master concludes : " That lizard, that crab, etc., will open for us the gates of paradise." Yet the scrupulous prophet, who saved lizards, must have held human life rather cheap, judging from the rivers of blood shed in his words. There are few so blood-thirsty as your really tender humanitarian. This credulity, this cheapness, this sentimentality, have left their mark in Hugo's poems. What could be more deplorable than the famous ass ?

> Cet âne abject, souillé, meutri sous le bâton
> Est plus saint que Socrate et plus grand que Platon.

" *LA LÉGENDE DES SIÈCLES* "

Or the bathos of this couplet—

> Un seul instant d'amour rouvre l'Eden fermé :
> Un porceau secouru pése un monde opprimé.

Both of which are mawkish lies.

Victor Hugo was a poetic demagogue. It was therefore no more possible for him to be sincere than it is for other demagogues. We must look in his works for the many magnificent passages when the poet spoke and the demagogue was silent.

XV

REMY DE GOURMONT

THE writer who approaches the task of estimating Remy de Gourmont's books may well be excused a certain shyness, for in him we have an exceedingly complex personality, nourished and developed by a vast knowledge of literature, expressing itself on very many subjects in different forms. Few men of letters can pretend to his erudition, so that to discuss the question of his literary filiation is in itself a most difficult task, and when to this is added the subtlety of his understanding, the variety of his topics, the paradox and irony of his writings, it will be seen that to form a just judgment is not easy. It is true that Gourmont is not an obscure author, though he was fond of praising obscurity in others ; there is nothing in his work which is not easily understood. That is not the difficulty. The difficulty lies rather in making a synthesis, in referring the utterances of this complex and sometimes contradictory mind to a guiding philosophy or principle. Gourmont spent

164

the best part of his life in writing and obviously wished very much to write well, yet he has produced no one supreme example of any of the forms of literature in which he worked. He was poet, novelist, literary critic, philosopher, translator, philologist, a student of biology, a skilled psychologist, and the possessor of a slowly evolved but beautiful and clear style. He is eminent as none of these, but remarkable because he possessed at once so many talents and accomplishments. He was second best at many things, for the reason that before he was a writer, before everything, he was " a lover of wisdom." He was a great man of letters and yet not that alone, for he used literature as an instrument to sharpen his intellect, to enable him to observe life widely and shrewdly. He did not believe in absolute truth, but he was a most scrupulous recorder of what he called " relative truth." He was not always consistent, but he was never a humbug, and his writings are filled with subtly noted points of psychology and remarks of deep wisdom. He was (it is an old simile) like an intellectual spider in the middle of a web of widely radiating interests. Action did not allure him (" l'homme d'action n'est qu'un terrassier ") ; he preferred to sit in his web of thought while the restless movement of life presented innumerable subjects for his reflection. The objects of his inquiries and reflections were most

165

various, from the Latin poetry of the Church to the finer points in the mentality of prostitutes; from the theories of Lucretius to the habits of insects; from the technique of *vers libre* to the philosophy of war. Yet his versatility never became amateurish.

The best and most thoughtful of Remy de Gourmont's novels is " Les Chevaux de Diomède." Much of his earlier work had a certain straining after effect, a desire for novelty at all costs, for fantastic ideas and complicated diction. He was then under the influence of curious, out-of-the-way literature. Gradually, however, and as if in spite of himself, he came to study more carefully the classics of his own and other countries; he evolved a style which was luminous and precise without losing any of his verve and personal originality. Style was always a preoccupation with him, and little by little he shed the factitious embellishments of his earlier work for a quieter but more beautiful sobriety. Style, which for the earlier Gourmont had been a kind of verbal gymnastics, became something more significant— " le style, c'est de sentir, de voir, de penser, et rien plus." " Diomède " was written at the time when he was beginning to see the comparative futility of a book like " Le Pèlerin du Silence." The characters in " Les Chevaux de Diomède " are not so much human personalities as abstractions, marionettes of flesh which move at their creator's whim. Fanette, Mauve, Néobelle, Cyrène are not living women but separate syntheses of feminine traits which provide Diomède (and Gourmont) with opportunities for making profound and often cynical remarks on human nature. None of Gourmont's novels can be read as a story; he was practically incapable of describing action, so that even when he does reluctantly make something happen, it is usually so commonplace that he has to take refuge in the not over-brilliant remark that " life is so like bad literature." Life is only like bad literature if we refuse to see it as anything else. Gourmont's detachment from life is in many ways a serious defect; though it does give serenity and wisdom to his writings, it renders him incapable of creating a vital character. His best work begins when the novelist is silent and the philosopher speaks. His intelligence, fine and pure as it was, seldom found its true method of expression, yet that intelligence is plain through all his earlier affectations, through even his most doubtful writing. He loved the human mind and yet he never really expressed that love. He is to be valued for his tranquil wisdom, for all the kindly or penetrating or ironic or beautiful thoughts which lie scattered through his books. He was a man of ideas and thoughts, not of complete works. Who can really care about the people in " Diomède " and yet who can fail to appreciate the subtlety of the scores of little remarks like these ?

> Les femmes ne sont vraiment belles que pour ceux qu'elles désirent.
>
> L'indulgence, c'est la forme aristocratique du dédain.
>
> J'estime qu'avec cinquante grognements gradués et autant de signes représentatifs, un troupeau d'hommes socialisés exprimera parfaitement tout son génie.
>
> Avez-vous remarqué, Pascase, la bonté de Dieu, et son infinie patience à modeler son âme divine sur l'âme humaine ?

Such *pensées* may or may not be just, but they force the reader to think. Perhaps that is why Remy de Gourmont never became widely popular ; he was always more interested in expressing some subtlety of thought than in entertaining his readers. His thought is a kind of pungent acid under whose action social humbugs and moral shams dissolve. Gourmont's irony was a deadly enemy to cant. He had no respect for institutions merely as such, nor was he ever intimidated by majorities ; indeed his errors come most frequently from his independence— any argument was good which could be used in defence of personal liberty. This profound love of freedom led him to a kind of philosophic anarchism, and yet he was not duped by his logic ; his intelligence was too wide, too far-seeing to become imprisoned in a system. The worst one can say of his philosophy is that it was highly artificial and was based on the existence of a safe and undisturbed life only ensured

to him by the condition of society he so freely criticized. A storm of violent action like the war threw
him at once off his balance ; it was some little time
before he recovered enough to write his detached
little fable about the warring ants.

Gourmont's constitutional inability to produce any
outstanding work made him an excellent commentator
on passing events. His articles were awaited with
interest by readers in many countries. And he was
a master of the " literary portrait," the short essay
which gathers into a few succinct paragraphs the
essential points of a writer's achievements. The two
volumes of the " Livres des masques " and the five
volumes of " Promenades littéraires " contain excellent judgments, not only on the writers of his own
generation but on many classic French and foreign
authors. A book like " Une Nuit au Luxembourg "
reveals not only a profound knowledge of Lucretius,
but shows the type of mind (rare enough) which
meditates another author to produce new ideas.
Gourmont never used literature with blind respect,
never clogged his mind with his acquisitions of
knowledge. Literature stimulated him and his mind
moved easily and freely under the weight of its
immense erudition. It may be said of him as of M.
Anatole France that to read him is a double pleasure
for the scholar, who will perceive many subtle
references and " over-tones," imperceptible to the

uninitiated. For years his writings were tinged with a particular flavour derived from the Latin prose and poetry of the Church. Where others read Racine and Hugo, Gourmont studied Gottschalcus, St. Ambrose, Adam of St. Victor, Notker, St. Bernard, and a multitude of similar authors. His book " Le Latin Mystique " is a revelation to those who have never ventured beyond classic Latin. When finally Gourmont came back to more modern studies his mind was in a state to see through the veil of familiarity which hides their beauty. He came to delight in Renaissance authors, and though he wrote against the classics he studied them and, what is more, understood them as few contemporary authors have done.

Gourmont, as might be expected, was not a success as a dramatist. In a play, incidental beauties, however remarkable, will not atone for lack of action. His poetry always tends to be rather a mosaic of coloured words than a cry of emotion or a swift dramatic moment. Yet there is charm in the sound of his " Litanies " and in the vague luxurious pictures they evoke. The chief value of Gourmont's writing is that it expresses a keen, delightful intelligence, one which was liable to error, but which possessed great subtlety and charm ; and that it expresses an exquisite and detached life which had about it nothing ignoble, mercenary, or base.

XVI

THE APPROACH TO M. MARCEL PROUST [1]

WHEN we speak of literary filiation we have frequently to make quite considerable mental reservations in the use of the term, for it is not so much the mere game of tracing influences which is involved as the implied definition of the artist's status, his relation not to the men of his own period but to his illustrious predecessors. Conducted with tact, the investigation is a kind of criticism ; it is, at any rate, a first means of approach. In the case of quite definitely minor intelligences—a Dowson or a Collins—men who have simply found a nugget or two in a mine previously worked by a more competent hand ; in such a case we can hardly talk of literary filiation in the precise sense. Here, if it is not a matter of imitation " pure and simple," it is at least a case where the smaller mind is self-ranked as such by its yielding to the greater. And in the case of sturdier minds which have achieved a certain some-

---

[1] Written before M. Proust's death.

thing which we yet know by instinct to be devoid
of distinction—a Wells or a Bourget—here again our
filiation is of small importance. It is like trying to
persuade ourselves that an agreeable *parvenu* has
the surface, the inimitable manner of some finished
example of the centuries' selection. But apply the
method to an *écrivain de race*, one who at least
appears to be in the grand line, and the result is
illuminating. Either we find that our subject is not
quite so fine as our enthusiasm proposed, a little
uneasy among the permanent residents of Parnassus,
or we discover that we have put down the outline
of a critical sketch. To establish these relationships,
these spiritual ancestries, as it were, is as important
to the student of literature as the correct tracing of
family descents is to an enthusiastic genealogist.
Of course no contemporary author can appear to us
with the prestige of those whose memories have
suffered from generations of incense burners. But the
mere fact of noting the filiation has its uses if only
those of introduction and of avoiding the merely
uncomparative method of criticism which leaves one
wondering whether the superlatives are superlatives
or only politenesses. It means that we are judging
an artist by his peers and implies the compliment
that we consider the immortals as such.
" Influences," as such, are uninteresting ; but it is
valuable to trace the main roots of a vigorous growth,

or, to vary the metaphor, to select an artist's spiritual affinities, the minds he would frequent in some ideal Elysium of the Landor kind.

As an artist M. Proust does nothing without significance ; or rather everything he does, even his use of the word " and," of a blank space, has a significance. His recent article on Flaubert in "La Nouvelle Revue Française" not only displayed a critical finesse which left one breathless, but revealed the writer's own methods, inasmuch as he was doing startling things with prose and achieving unheard of subtleties. It is hardly fantastic to see in M. Proust's "Pastiches" not so much a set of parodies which would rank above even a brilliant book like "A Christmas Garland," as a statement, oblique but unmistakable, of his literary filiation. There may be a further significance in the fact that this book is dedicated to an American, which is at least piquant and suggestive. I feel almost sure that in publishing these elaborate essays in the styles of his predecessors —pastiches which are at once a criticism and an homage—M. Proust had the intention of showing us a few of the writers from the study of whom he has built up his own unique style and something of the fabric of his thought. Balzac, Flaubert, Sainte-Beuve, Henri de Régnier, the Goncourts, Michelet, Faguet, Renan, and Saint-Simon—this is at once a formidable list of " great names " and, if the phrase

173

may be used without impropriety, a somewhat heterogeneous paternity for an artist. Yet the list is by no means complete, for we must add to it the name of an Englishman—let the super-modern reader prepare to start—John Ruskin, and probably Chateaubriand and Mallarmé.

I see I was right to speak of that list as " formidable," not because of the implied pretentiousness, but because of the very elaborate analyses which would become necessary if these relationships were minutely discussed. The responsibility may be thrown on M. Proust ; he is not only an elaborate artist but the cause of elaboration in others. His work is perhaps the most complex literary " problem " of this decade ; it is certainly the most fascinating. But I can do no more than hint at the immense opportunities for literary analysis which I see in this problem. To pursue them at all far would involve me in endless subtleties. Yet one or two suggestions may be usefully made.

It will be noted that only five of the first ten artists named were novelists ; the others were historians, critics, philosophers, and writers of memoirs. This is significant, for if M. Proust is first of all a novelist of tremendous ability, he is also an acute critic, a philosopher in morals, and a writer of contemporary history. His work is the first attempt at a synthesis of modern European civilization,

THE APPROACH TO MARCEL PROUST

localized at a point of intensity. It is this attempt
(and its success), one of the many motives of the
million-word " A la Récherche du Temps Perdu,"
which gives the volumes which have appeared their
first startling importance. The book has so many
roots, so many intentions ; it is packed so full of
meaning, of thought, and observation, that it is a
kind of literature in itself.

The writer of memoirs, of contemporary social
history, is conspicuous in M. Proust. If this side of
varied talent links him partly to Balzac it also proves
a closer filiation with Saint-Simon. It is not the
modern habit of decrying Balzac which causes me to
set M. Proust above him in this particular ; it is
because M. Proust has a conception of the art which
places him, lower indeed than Saint-Simon, but
in Saint-Simon's class. Balzac too often wrote as
a woman acts ; from intuition. His observations on
social life, his attempts at an epitome of the civilization he lived in, are generally brilliant guesses,
sometimes rather ridiculous guesses. Saint-Simon,
with his more restricted purpose, enjoyed the advantages of really knowing the life he described and the
characters he analysed. The creative value of his
work is not greater than Balzac's, it is not even more
voluminous, but it has that sense of reality which is
the gift of intimacy alone (in comparison with which
Balzac's writing appears like that of an art-critic

insufficiently educated in pictures), it has so many of those details and shades of meaning which are the life of memoirs. To speak of Saint-Simon in the terms of a French Pepys, as an English critic recently did, is an enormity of bad taste and insensitiveness. The likeness is that of a well to a lake. M. Proust, with his extreme sensitiveness in critical perceptions, understands perfectly the significance of Saint-Simon as an artist, in sharp distinction to his significance as an author of documents which time has invested with interest. M. Proust has studied and used Saint-Simon's methods in rendering his own observations of modern life. And merely because they are observations of modern life M. Proust's writings have a more intimate if less stately and imposing meaning for us. The complicated but perfectly controlled knowledge, the enthusiasm for a " situation " which Saint-Simon put into the discussion of some problem of precedence, some Court manœuvre, are devoted by M. Proust to the modern interests of psychological analysis, a nuance of sentiment, a delicate relationship, an appreciation of some fine distinction. When he describes so minutely the exact manner and air in which Swann raised his hat during a certain period of his life, or renders that amazing dinner-party with M. de Norpois, M. Proust is definitely doing for his age and generation what Saint-Simon did for his. The conditions, the " data,"

176

of the problem are all changed ; the method is the same. It is M. Proust's misfortune that he is dealing in fact—in spite of certain exceptions which remain like fine old houses in a modern street—only with a luxurious bourgeoisie, preoccupied essentially with what is " chic " as distinct from what is really cultured. He feels the lack of an established aristocracy, which was so precious an asset to Saint-Simon. And inasmuch as M. Proust's own intelligence is aristocratic, he is an anachronism. He suffers in the same way as Renan, who could never find a place in an omnibus because he was too polite to precede another passenger. He lacks that ordered state of society where an exquisite refinement of this kind is foreseen and compensated by privileges.

I do not wish to create the feeling that M. Proust is a pompous or intolerably refined person, though I can see a line of argument which could represent him merely as the most astonishing case of neurasthenia which ever existed. But in each case his manners are too good for him to be any of these. His sensitiveness, that habit of mind which can be described only by the misused " cultured," is something so intimate, so unforced, and yet so controlled that the personality disengaged from his books becomes something typical and representative, an ideal presentation of the best in the old world as Whitman, in another sense, was of the new. The

M   177

complaints directed against M. Proust's amorously detailed analyses and the inordinately long curves of his thought are unjustified. M. Proust is neither a pompous nor a wordy writer. Unhesitatingly one can point to Flaubert as his closest predecessor, and he shares with Flaubert that salt of irony which makes " Bonvard et Pécuchet " one of the world's great satires. M. Proust has assimilated Flaubert's methods and even refined on them. One can trace the Flaubert manner throughout his pages, not as an " influence " but as a similar habit of mind. In some respects even M. Proust's gigantic novel is a new, more detailed " Education Sentimentale." M. Proust has a conception of his art as high as Flaubert's. Their minds are the same kind of diamond, but whereas Flaubert's was shaped in a few facets, M. Proust's glitters innumerably. He is in some respects a Flaubert indefinitely elaborated. And his highly complex form of narrative should have no difficulties for those who have assimilated Ulysses and Mary Olivier and Miriam's interminable impressions. M. Proust is more coherent than Mr. Joyce, more urbane, less preoccupied with slops and viscera. His scale is more gigantic than anything Miss Sinclair has yet attempted. And he is not merely an impressionist like Miss Richardson. He can be an impressionist, a marvellous impressionist when necessary, he can use that almost fabulous virtuosity one admires in

THE APPROACH TO MARCEL PROUST

Miss Richardson's work, but he can do so many
things more. You could furnish a new Rochefoucauld
and another volume to Montaigne from his pages.
With all one's good will, one cannot say that of Miss
Richardson. And though M. Proust can describe a
public convenience with a precision and verve which
would have aroused the jealousy even of Flaubert,
he is devoid of that acrid Tertullian-like spirit which,
in Mr. Joyce, makes one uneasily conscious that he
is engaged in the moral vulgarity of disparaging the
universe. M. Proust has the urbanity, the fine
manners Nature denied to Mr. Joyce when she gave
him genius ; he has the vast scheme of civilizations
which Miss Sinclair has not yet tried to render ;
he has a significance we look for in vain in Miss
Richardson.

M. Proust's admiration for Ruskin is one of the
typical, distinctive characteristics of his mind. It
is not the affected admiration for Ruskin's " purple
periods," which Wilde professed, and it is certainly
not a sympathy for Ruskin's views on art. It is an
admiration directed towards Ruskin's essential appre-
ciativeness, his capacity for the assimilation and
understanding of beauty, his reverence for the arts
as symbols and expressions of civilization. Often,
especially in modern Paris, you will find an art looked
upon as something self-supporting, as if it had an
existence of its own, independent of the civilization

179

in which it lives and by which it should be nourished and of the past from which it grew. This error, which is being cleverly though perhaps unconsciously exposed by the Dadaistes, leads inevitably to death, and is profoundly repulsive to M. Proust. We can observe it in a thousand little points of his writing. He finds it as unpleasant to repudiate a dead artist as he would the memory of a relative. Perhaps one of the most useful things proved by his books is that a mind steeped in tradition, a mind almost fastidiously respectful, has nevertheless created one of the most original novels of the time.

XVII

THE POETRY OF T. S. ELIOT

TO define twentieth-century literature when it is only beginning to emerge is a feat one may be excused from attempting. But one may note a certain homogeneity in the writings of M. Marcel Proust and Mr. James Joyce, of Miss Sitwell and Mr. Huxley, of Miss Moore and H. D., of Jean Cocteau and Paul Morand and T. S. Eliot. They are intellectually contemporaries ; they are post-war ; they are sufficiently unlike each other to reward curiosity and sufficiently similar to show the first oultine of a period. The typical modern poet whose affinities are chiefly with the writers above mentioned is something extremely unlike the conventional idea of a poet. Some day, when the first authoritative collection of writings by these poets is issued, the editor should put as an epigraph two quotations from " Une Saison en Enfer "—

Quant au bonheur établi, domestique ou non . . . non, je ne peux pas.

LITERARY STUDIES AND REVIEWS

Je vais dévoiler tous les mystères : mystères réligieux ou naturels, mort, naissance, avenir, passé, cosmogonie, néant. Je suis maître en fantasmagories.

This (hypothetical) modern poet is not amiable or romantic or tender or tranquil ; but neither is the age in which he lives. And as irreverence and indocility are qualities of this decade, so are they of this decade's poets. The platoons of poets " going through the motions " of verse in unison at the word of some invisible commander are superannuated for ever. The new poet is the " poète contumace " of Laforgue. His indocility is extreme and nearly as disturbing to the godly as his determination to accept none of the official wax effigies as realities, to take nothing seriously until it has been proved worthy of seriousness. His thought is pessimistic and disillusioned ; his modes of expression sarcastic and his chief weapon an acrid wit. He is psychologically subtle and intellectually acute ; his culture is extensive. He is not a democrat though he observes popular habits. He is a cosmopolitan, but he enjoys the flavour of nationality. He writes for an audience equipped to understand him, and is indifferent to popular success. His mind is exceedingly complex and moves with a rapidity incomprehensible to sluggish wits. He is perilously balanced among the rude forces of a turbulent mechanical age ; he walks the tight-rope over an

182

THE POETRY OF T. S. ELIOT

abyss and he knows it. His work has the gusto of peril.

The works of Mr. James Joyce may be taken as typical of the best original prose of this school; the poetry of Mr. Eliot occupies a similar position. The plan of this article forbids discussion of Mr. Eliot's criticism, but it is essential to observe that the faculty of analysis which makes the " Sacred Wood " so valuable is equally characteristic of " Prufrock " and " Ara vos prec." When Mr. Eliot analyses as a critic he clarifies one's ideas, enlarges one's comprehension, purifies one's taste. And the author of the " Sacred Wood " is of one piece with the author of " Ara vos prec." That is a conclusion not to be dodged. You cannot accept the " Sacred Wood " and ignore Mr. Eliot's poetry; each is a different facet of the same talent; and that talent cannot be disposed of by a little cheap journalism. As a character in one of Mr. Eliot's poems says, interpreting so strangely well one's sensation of his thoroughness and impeccable restraint, his strength of purpose—

> You are invulnerable, you have no Achilles' heel.
> You will go on, and when you have prevailed
> You can say : at this point many a one has failed.

The reader will almost certainly have noticed that when the syllables " T. S. Eliot " are pronounced, the reply " Laforgue " is elicited as invariably as an automatic machine produces a very small piece of chocolate when pressed with a penny. Now it is certainly true that Mr. Eliot's poetry has some affinity with Laforgue's poetry ; but is it not a perfect example of muddled thinking to deduce imitation from affinity of mind, just as the same muddled thought deduces affinity of mind from imitation ? Is it not certain that such people have never worked out even this simple distinction ? And yet, with so faulty an equipment, they will undertake to analyse a work as profound and complex as " Ara vos prec." To say that Mr. Eliot imitates Laforgue because they have a common faculty for unexpected juxtapositions of ideas expressed with ironic wit is as foolish as it would be to say that Mr. Eliot imitates Ausonius because both frequently quote other poets in their verse. Moreover, Mr. Eliot has quite as much affinity with Rimbaud and Corbière. Mr. Eliot's " Mélange adultère de tout " depends for its full effect upon the reader's comprehending the reference to Corbière's " Épave mort-né." But Mr. Eliot has completely purged out Corbière's querulous romanticism and self-pity; he is hard on himself—

> En Amérique, professeur ;
> En Angleterre, journaliste ;
> C'est à grands pas et en sueur
> Que vous suivrez à peine ma piste.

THE POETRY OF T. S. ELIOT

En Yorkshire, conférencier ;
A Londres, un peu banquier ;
(Vous me paierez bien la tête.)
C'est à Paris que je me coiffe
Casque noir de jemenfoutiste.
En Allemagne, philosophe
Surexcité par Emporheben
Au grand air de Bergsteigleben ;
J'erre toujours de-ci de-là
A divers coups de tra-la-la
De Damas jusqu'à Omaha ;
Je célébrai mon jour de fête
Dans un oasis d'Afrique
Vêtu d'une peau de girafe.

On montrera mon cénotaphe
Aux côtes brûlants de Mozambique.

The intention of parody, the reference to Verlaine,
the compression, the tone of badinage in which the
experiences of a varied life are dismissed, are
characteristic of the modern poet All Mr. Eliot's
poems in French fit in perfectly with the development
of the younger French poets. The tone of disillusion
of " Lune de Miel " and the singular dialogue with
a dirty waiter, called " Dans le Restaurant," would
be highly approved by our " chers confrères." At
least we may be certain that he would be greeted
as a poet by the author of the following lines, whose
inferiority to those of Mr. Eliot is apparent—

Voyez le vieux Goethe ; il sautille
Comme une chèvre sur le Vésuve ;

> Il porte un livre grec, un herbier,
> Un filet à papillons ;
> Il casse des gros morceaux de Vésuve
> Et en rempli ses poches,
> Car la fin des vacances d'Eckermann
> Approche . . . etc.

It is not a question of imitation or even of similarity of manner, but of having reached a similar stage of intelligence.

Mr. Eliot's English poetry is often attacked as incomprehensible and heartless ; which is simply another way of saying that it is subtle and not sentimental. His desire for perfection is misrepresented as puritan and joyless, whereas it is plain he discriminates in order to increase his enjoyment. But, of course, refinement will not be applauded by those who cannot perceive it, nor will intelligence be appreciated by those who cannot understand it ; literary criticism is not the only human activity wherein ignorance is made a standard. Mr. Eliot's poetry makes very high demands on a reader's intelligence and knowledge. It is caviare to the general. And yet this poetry can at once be assimilated into tradition, may be placed at once as the last development of two currents of thought, one French and the other English. The common perception of the affinity between " Ara vos prec " and " Les Complaintes " may be extended to " Les Illuminations " and " Les Amours Jaunes." And when the reader has granted that, he has simply admitted that one side of Mr. Eliot's poetry is a development of the secular tradition of " poètes contumaces " or " poètes libertins," which runs from the poets of to-day to Laforgue and Verlaine, to Rimbaud and Corbière, to Aloysius Bertrand, to Saint-Amant, to Théophile, back to Villon, and beyond him to a shadowy host of mediæval " pinces-sans-rire," " goliards " and satiric " goguenards," whose sharp tongues spared neither the Church nor the rich nor the pretty ladies. That tradition of poignant, witty, derisive verse has survived many centuries and passed through many transformations ; it has been stifled underground for a generation or more, but has always sprung up in some new form— that sharp French mind whose watchword is " ne pas être dupe." So that when we find in Mr. Eliot agreeable sarcasms of this sort—

> The sable presbyters approach
> The avenue of penitence ;
> The young are red and pustular,
> Clutching piaculative pence,

our mind runs at once to

> Sur mol duvet assis, ung gros chanoine,

and

> Ce fanfaron de Ferradine,
> Qui pare son affreuse mine
> D'un grand et vilain chifreneau,
> Aura beau tordre ses bigottes,
> Beau renasquer à hautes nottes, etc.

187

If the reader will take the trouble to spend a few days with the poets quoted he will appreciate the point at issue. It is not required to prove that these generations of poets imitated each other, but simply that they belong to a category of the intelligence which has produced remarkable poetry and shown extraordinary persistence and vitality.

When this aspect of Mr. Eliot's poetry is explained, there remains the more serious and difficult problem of his so-called obscurity. Now the charge of " obscurity " may be just, for all verse which on analysis proves to have no intellectual or emotional content is " obscure "; obscure because it pretends to possess a meaning which it has not. But the obscurity of Mr. Eliot is as much a myth of lazy people as the obscurity of Browning. Indeed, Mr. Eliot's verse never makes the heavy demands on a reader that were made by " Sordello." But this subtlety of mind which makes necessary an effort for full comprehension is not something invented by Browning, but goes far beyond him to the so-called metaphysical poets, to Donne and Davies and Chapman. Compare the following paragraphs—

> History has many cunning passages, contrived corridors
> And issues ; deceives with whispering ambitions,
> Guides us by vanities. Think now
> She gives when our attention is distracted,
> And what she gives, gives with such supple confusions
> That the giving famishes the craving. Gives too late

THE POETRY OF T. S. ELIOT

> What's not believed in, or if still believed
> In memory only, reconsidered passion. Gives too soon
> Into weak hands what's thought can be dispensed with
> Till the refusal propagates a fear.
>
> Oh, of what contraries consists a man !
> Of what impossible mixtures ! vice and virtue,
> Corruption and eterness, at one time,
> And in one subject, let together, loose !
> We have not any strength but weakens us,
> No greatness but doth crush us into air.
> Our knowledges do light us but to err,
> Our ornaments are burthens : our delights
> Are our tormentors ; fiends that, raised in fears
> At parting shake our roofs about our ears.

Is there so great disparity between the modern and the Elizabethan ? Does not the modern poet speak with the accents of his great predecessors, though the matter of his speech be remote from theirs ? Is it not certain that this feigned obscurity is no obscurity, but simply density of thought ?

If space and the patience of readers permitted, there would be a great pleasure in carrying these comparisons into every aspect of Mr. Eliot's poetry. Let us take but one more instance where the modern poet and the poets of the seventeenth century have " unveiled death," have forced themselves to look unmoved on dreadful horrors—

> . . . saw the skull beneath the skin ;
> And breastless creatures underground
> Leaned backward with a lipless grin.

189

Daffodil bulbs instead of balls
Stared from the sockets of the eyes !
He knew that thought clings round dead limbs
Tightening its lusts and luxuries.

What that ?   O, fatal ! he throws earth upon me !
A dead man's skull beneath the roots of flowers !

I prithee, yet remember,
Millions are now in graves which at last day
Like mandrakes shall rise shrieking.

. . . they'll re-marry
Ere the worm pierce your winding-sheet, ere the spider
Make a thin curtain for your epitaphs.

Or as sometimes in a beheaded man,
Though at those two red seas which freely ran,
One from the trunk, another from the head,
His soul be sail'd to her eternal bed,
His eyes will twinkle, and his tongue will roll,
As though he beck'ned and call'd back his soul. . . .

It is a long step from the dense thought of **Mr. Eliot's** " Gerontion " and the sombre horrors of his " Whispers of Immortality " to the pleasant little rhymes now current. Between these rhymes, however pretty and melodious, and the intellectual poetry of Mr. Eliot, there is a wide gulf. Few will contest the originality of the mind expressed in his poetry, and yet the comparisons instituted show that Mr. Eliot's poetry is traditional, linking up on the one hand with the ironic French poets and, on the other, with the stately, subtle-minded Englishmen of the Renaissance. The poetry of **Mr. T. S.**

THE POETRY OF T. S. ELIOT

Eliot is a healthy reaction against the merely pretty and agreeable, against shallowness and against that affectation of simplicity which verged on dotage. Mr. Eliot is to be honoured as a poet who has brought new vigour to the intellectual tradition of English poetry.[1]

[1] Written before the publication of "Waste Land." I have been censured by an old friend for mixing quotations from Mr. Eliot and the Elizabethans, without indicating the authors. My object is merely to surprise the reader into admitting how "traditional" this "revolutionary" poet is.

XVIII

MR. JAMES JOYCE'S " ULYSSES "

" La vie n'est de soy ny bien ny mal ; c'est la place du bien et du mal, selon que vous la leur faictes."

MONTAIGNE:

I

MR. JOYCE'S " Ulysses " is most interesting both for its achievement and for the influence it must have ; the achievement I am convinced is remarkable, its influence, I fear, may be deplorable. If young writers could be persuaded to applaud and honour Mr. Joyce without copying him, all would be well ; but such a thing is unlikely. It is part of the charm of youth that it wishes to resemble those it admires ; but who can feel anything but perturbed at the idea of a whole crop of pseudo-Joyce prose writers ? From the manner of Mr. Joyce to Dadaisme is but a step and from Dadaisme to imbecility is hardly that. Where Mr. Joyce has succeeded, with occasional lapses, others must fail, lacking his intellectuality, his amazing observation, memory, and intuition, his control over the processes of his art

192

MR. JAMES JOYCE'S "ULYSSES"

Mr. Joyce is a modern Naturaliste, possessing a greater knowledge of intimate psychology, but without the Naturaliste preoccupation with "l'écriture artiste." He is less conscious, more intuitive than the Naturalistes; if the expression is not too strained, he has made realism mystic. "Dubliners," influenced by French writers, was a book to which Zola would have given his "nihil obstat." It was neither better nor worse than a great many French Naturaliste books; the stories in "Dubliners" were very nearly the sort of thing that Octave Mirbeau has written. The book attracted attention for the reason that Naturalisme was a literary mode little practised by writers of English fiction who were also artists. I have no doubt that quantities of so-called realistic novels have been published in England and America in the last thirty years, but the true Naturaliste genre has been rarely exploited with success. I suppose Gissing was an English Naturaliste. Neither James nor Mr. George Moore nor Mr. Conrad is a Naturaliste in the sense that Mirbeau, Hennique, Zola, the earlier Huysmans and even the Goncourts (in "La Fille Elisa" and "Germinie Lacerteux") were Naturalistes. "Dubliners" was plainly related to these French novels. The object of the Naturalistes was to produce a "slice of life," preferably as sordid and as repulsive as possible. Thus "La Fille Elisa" (E. de Goncourt) is the wretched life story of a criminal prostitute; "Contes de la Chaumière" (Mirbeau) are sketches of peasant life, where every character is depraved, vicious, and ugly; "A Vau l'Eau" (Huysmans) is the history of a bilious Government clerk who spends his life trying to purchase a decent meal in Paris, and of course without success. The "philosophy" of the Naturalistes was sombre and derisive; they were exceedingly pessimistic; they held that life is a most wretched experience, that happiness is impossible, and mankind destitute of virtue. They divided men into the poor and the rich. The poor endured lives of desolating banality, poisoned with bad alcohol and worse food, brutalized by excessive labour, stunted by poverty, devastated by the passions of greed, hatred, and lust, which last almost invariably gave them venereal disease. The rich dragged out a bored existence in crass and stupid luxury, agitated by much the same passions, equally unhappy, and almost equally diseased. If the characters of a Naturaliste novel were in the country, it was invariably winter or else perpetually raining (as in Swinburne's depressed "Ballade of Burdens"); if they lived in towns they were pursued by evil smells, smoke, and bad air, and frequently contracted tuberculosis. All this was "rendered" with extraordinary talent and verve; the style of men like Edmond de Goncourt is original and exquisite, and who needs to

194

be reminded of the beautiful clarity of Maupassant's prose ?

"Dubliners" was an excellent example of the Naturaliste method in English fiction. It was written carefully and in fine precise prose; the characters were nearly all inhabitants of the worst Dublin slums, and their lives were unfortunate, dismal, and usually depraved. It was objective, according to the Naturaliste method. The writer "presented" his characters without comment; he did not reflect or moralize. But in "Dubliners," as in the writings of French Naturalistes, a didactic purpose was plain, all protests to the contrary. This purpose was to show that life for the majority of human beings is more or less disgusting, that the deepest passions are perverted and debased by the conditions imposed by society, that men are selfish, beastly, domineering when they have power, cringing when they are weak; above all, that men and women are singularly nasty when moved by sexual emotions. Perhaps I put it a little strongly, but that is my impression on re-reading the French Naturalistes, and it coincides with my memory of "Dubliners." After "Dubliners" Mr. Joyce issued the "Portrait of the Artist as a Young Man." This was at once an original achievement and a departure from conventional Naturaliste methods. It was autobiographical and not objective. It was the life story of Stephen Daedalus who, to use the writer's own words, was " a sensitive nature smarting under the lashes of an undivined and squalid way of life." This book, issued unpretentiously and in the midst of the war, caused considerable discussion and aroused enthusiasm in men of letters " open " to new impressions and admirations. The " Portrait " was certainly "squalid," but it had magnificent qualities. No such pitiless and close analysis of adolescence has been written in recent years ; the numerous other autobiographical novels seemed mere egotistic self-glorification beside it. Moreover, the observation of character, remarkable enough in " Dubliners," was here triumphant and masterly. Stephen at home, Stephen at school, Stephen growing up in the agonies of adolescence, Stephen in his relations with other young men and girls, was portrayed with skill and insight. Those who pretended not to admire the book must have been very dull or very malignant. Undoubtedly the " triumph " of large sales and the admiration of silly women were not forthcoming, but Mr. Joyce had the admiration and respect of almost all his contemporaries and many of his elders. His next book was awaited with great interest. This proved to be " Ulysses."

MR. JAMES JOYCE'S " ULYSSES "

II

Consider for a moment Mr. Joyce's position in
the interval between " The Portrait " and " Ulysses."
He appeared to have outgrown the immature
Naturalisme of " Dubliners " and had certainly
improved immensely as a writer of fiction. True
" The Portrait " was sordid, but it had fine passages ;
the contest between the " idealism " of Daedalus
and the outer world of crass stupidity and ugliness
was very moving. The spiritual conflict lifted the
story out of squalor into tragedy, though there
was a lingering over unsavoury details which spoiled
the balance of the book. It was nasty in many
spots, but with a kind of tonic nastiness. One felt
that here was a man of extreme sensitiveness and
talent getting rid of " perilous stuff," throwing
off the evil dreams and influences of mawkish youth
to reach a saner, clearer view of human life. Many
people must have had great hopes of Mr. Joyce. I
did not for one moment desire him to accept a particle
of the official optimism which is so poisonous ; I
did not want him to be " sugary " or to affect a
Renanesque benevolence and calm which were
obviously foreign to his character. But I did hope
to see him write real tragedy and not return to
the bastard genre of the Naturalistes who mingle
satire and tragedy and produce something wholly

197

false ; I hoped to see his characters emerge into a clearer air from the sordid arena in which they were subdued by Fate in a debris of decayed vegetables and putrid exhalations.

Clearly I hoped the wrong thing. " Ulysses " is more bitter, more sordid, more ferociously satirical than anything Mr. Joyce has yet written. It is a tremendous libel on humanity which I, at least, am not clever enough to refute, but which I am convinced is a libel. There is laughter in " Ulysses," but it is a harsh, sneering kind, very different from the " gros rire " of Rabelais. I see that Mr. Pound, champion of " Ulysses," abuses Tertullian ; but is not Mr. Joyce a modern Tertullian and worse ? In my " Mella Patraum " I can find nothing of Tertullian which shows such repugnance for humanity, which teaches such abhorrence of the human body, and particularly of sexual relations, as I find in " Ulysses." Some people find Mr. Joyce " indecent and repulsive " ; repulsive, he may be, if you believe in human happiness, human goodness, and human relations. But not indecent in any seductive sense. He is no Laclos or Crébillon fils. He reminds me of St. Bernard discoursing of the horror of death : " Tunc veniet corpus in pallorem et horrorem, in saniem et fetorem ; erit vermis et cibus vermium." Or again most strongly of Odo of Cluny, when he abuses women foully : " If men could see beneath

198

the skin . . . the very sight of women would be disgusting to them. Consider what is hidden in women's nostrils, in their throats, in their stomachs : filth everywhere. . . . And we who would not touch with our finger-tips vomit or dung—how can we long to clasp in our arms a mere bag of excrements ! " Transpose the urbanities of these holy men into the " tone " of Bloom's meditations, and who would not swear they were passages from " Ulysses " ? Ought we to allow our admiration for Mr. Joyce's talents to blind us to the falsity of his views on life ? Certainly not all the sanctity of Odo and Bernard will ever make me forgive them their " Naturalisme." After all, this is a false view of life unless suicide be our aim. Logically I see no end to " Ulysses " except the suicide of Bloom, though no doubt it will terminate in the pleasant purlieus of a public lavatory.

Every artist is perfectly free to advance his own theories of life, however far he may wander from the sublime mediocrities of truth. And indeed there is so much that is true in " Ulysses " that to pick out the false from the true would be a lengthy process. All I wish to say now is that I think Mr. Joyce overstresses certain aspects of existence which most writers foolishly ignore, that he tries to convince us that life is less attractive than we had thought, even in our most depressed moods.

I remember reading one of the " Episodes " more than two years ago in a front-line trench, and I think the situation was most appropriate. There indeed were vile smells, abrupt nerve-racking noises, dirt and disease ; life was confined to a dismal hide and seek with annihilation ; the conveniences, the amenities of existence were reduced to the compass of a large hole underground ; lack of sleep, nerves, monotonous diet, no baths had made us all fit subjects for Mr. Joyce's sneers and satire. We, whom the noisy voices of two continents vaunted as heroes, by a singular irony were no more than a red-eyed, muddy, unshaved set of " pitiful rascals " puddling along duck-boards, crawling among shell-holes and rusty wire, dodging ferocious instruments of death, wholly absorbed in the problem of how to live until the next relief, and completely depressed by the impossibility of escape. But were we despicable ? Had we poor infantry cannon-fodder —apt symbols of humanity in a world whose misery seems to have neither purpose nor justification—had we nothing to set against our grotesque sufferings ? Let those answer " No " who never knew the comradeship of the front line, who never saw a man give his life for another, who never shared that dumb profound kindness of common men under a mutual disaster. I knew that comradeship ; I knew an obscure soldier who lay out under a heavy barrage to give

the comfort of his presence to two wounded men,
though he could easily have escaped to safety and
was indeed ordered to do so ; I have known an
officer lose his life to save his servant's. And I
say that such things, obscure, unknown, show that
men are not wholly debased even by the disgusting
savagery of war, that they can be equally superior
in the disgusting vulgarities of daily existence. I
say, moreover, that when Mr. Joyce, with his
marvellous gifts, uses them to disgust us with
mankind, he is doing something which is false
and a libel on humanity.

That is my opinion of Mr. Joyce's " Ulysses." It
is opinion, I know, not criticism, and doubtless I
shall be called everything from " banal " to " sentimental " for expressing it, but it is better to be
thought sentimental than to acquire by falsity a
reputation for brilliance. From the point of view
of art there is some justification for Mr. Joyce ;
he has succeeded in writing a most remarkable
book ; but from the point of view of human life
I am sure he is wrong. Moreover, the style of
" Ulysses," which Mr. Joyce usually handles success-
fully, will be as deplorably false in his imitators as
his philosophy. " Ulysses " is a gigantic soliloquy.
Bloom is a kind of rags and tatters Hamlet, a
proletarian Lear, " mirroring " life and showing it
to be hideous. Mr. Joyce has pushed the intimate

detailed analysis of character to a point farther than
any writer I know. His faithful reproduction of
Bloom's thoughts, with their inconsequence, their
staccato breaks, their returns to an obsession, is
an astonishing psychological document. The telegraphic method is there apt and justified. And
there is also a good artistic reason for the abandon-
ment of all unity of prose tone, a unity always
observed by the French Naturalistes. Sometimes
Mr. Joyce writes journalese; sometimes a kind
of prose poetry; sometimes a rapid narrative;
often the telegraphic prose of Bloom's thoughts;
occasionally he is deliberately obscene; too often
he is incoherent. Yet in nearly every case he
achieves his " effect." He has done daring but
quite wonderful things with words. He can be
sober, ironic, disgusting, platitudinous, sarcastic,
realistic, just as he wishes. He has telescoped
drama with narrative and varies the tone of his
narrative to suit the dramatic situation. He is
no longer objective, no more the detached narrator;
he wishes to identify himself with his subject and
to identify both with the reader. It is this which
makes me say he has made realism mystic. He
has lost the sense of mental boundaries; his writing
is a sort of self-abandonment, a merging of his
consciousness in that of others. I am no philosopher
to explain this process, but I am certain it has

202

occurred and that M. Julien Benda could analyse it perfectly and pitilessly. In Mr. Joyce it is acceptable because he does dominate it, just as his singular prose is readable because he controls it completely; but imagine this peculiar mysticism degenerated into mere sloppiness and loose thinking, imagine this heterogeneous style degenerated into incoherence, affectation, and wordy confusion, and then think what will be the result of Mr. Joyce's influence. I attach no overwhelming importance to the Dadaistes; as I am reminded, they have not managed to destroy M. Anatole France; but a whole generation of Dada in England and America would be rather deplorable. If the Dadaistes wish to destroy literature by making it ridiculous (as they have declared) they are welcome to try; but I think they should not be encouraged. Yet Mr. Joyce with his great undisciplined talent is more dangerous than a shipload of Dadaistes. Young writers will be dominated by his personality; they will copy his eccentricities instead of developing their own minds. If only we could treat Mr. Joyce as Plato recommends; give him praise and anoint him with oil and put a crown of purple wool on his head and send him into another country.

III

There is no art without originality; there is no originality without personality. And a man's personality is developed, altered, moulded as much by the books he reads as by the friends he frequents. A man's library reveals him nearly as much as his wife. Imitation in art nearly always results in falsity; it is the curse of modern culture. Academic literature, founded on imitation of classic and accepted writers, is notoriously pallid and boring; "radical" literature, founded on the imitation of the eccentricities of new writers, is incoherent, vapid, and often imbecile   A style which is allusive, derived, full of quotations, is a bad style because it is pedantic and lifeless; and a style which is affected, strained for effect, incomprehensible, is a bad style because the only reason for using words is to make ourselves understood.   Merely to astonish simple-minded people with profound-looking imbecilities is not literature; it is playing the fool in print.   But though all conscious or unconscious imitation of other writers is a literary vice, there is a perfectly real and useful influence in the frequentation of good books.   I do not think it any praise to say that a man writes as if he had never read a book; I should think it was praise to say he had read a great many good books and that he wrote without imitating them, but trained and polished by their example. Imitations of Shakespeare are always repulsive and absurd, but it is certain that because of Shakespeare, the greatest English poets have a verbal richness and imagination almost unknown in French poetry. A man who imitates the gestures or copies the witticisms of his friends is rightly despised; but we do not despise a man who is formed and enlightened by contact with the world. The same may be said of a writer and the books he frequents, for they too are friends not to be imitated but studied. We should not advise a young man who wished to acquire a knowledge of life to spend all his time between Mile End and the East India Dock; it would be just as foolish to confine a young writer to Rimbaud, Dostoievsky, and Mr. Joyce, who, I believe, are " it " in advanced circles. A prose style founded on Tacitus and Madame de Sévigné could not be vulgar though it might be lifeless, could not be incoherent though it might be insipid. And the tendency of modern literature—I mean the experimental, non-commercial kind—is towards vulgarity and incoherence and away from distinction and sobriety.

I have not wandered from Mr. Joyce. His influence, which I dare to prophesy will be considerable, cannot be a wholly good one. He is disgusting with a reason;" others will be disgusting without reason. He is obscure and justifies his obscurity; but how many others will write mere confusion and think it sublime? How many dire absurdities will be brought forth, with "Ulysses" as midwife? Mr. Joyce himself is little influenced by his contemporaries, though he is obviously steeped in Church writers, the classics, and French literature. He has read the Russians perhaps more than is good for him. But he is not one of those superficial people who pick up some shallow artifice as the canon of a new form of art; he will be the prey of coteries, but he himself is far above them. I recall an interesting remark of M. Marcel Proust. He says that Hugo was deep in Dion Cassius and Tacitus when he was at his most Romantic, that M. Denis was daily at the Louvre while producing his most individual pictures. I have myself met Gaudier Brzeska prowling furtively about the Elgin marbles. New art, says M. Proust, is for the public, but classic art is for the artists. The young writer should not neglect his contemporaries, but his chief companions ought to be the classics. "Ulysses" is dangerous reading for anyone whose style is unformed. If I had a younger friend who wanted to write and would accept my advice, I would conceal from him the works of Mr. Joyce and set him on Pascal and Voltaire, with Mr. George Moore and Flaubert as light reading. And when he knew the

value of clarity, sobriety, precision—the good
manners of literature—I would hand him Mr.
Joyce's books with the highest eulogy and little
fear of the consequences.[1]

[1] This note was written before "Ulysses" was published in
book-form. That event has not greatly modified my opinions,
except to convince me that "Ulysses" is the grave-stone, the
cromlech, of Naturalisme. I am happy to recognize that the influence of "Ulysses" in England has been microscopic; perhaps
that was because everyone concentrated on the last chapter and
ignored the remarkable phantasmagoria two chapters earlier.

XIX

THE POET AND HIS AGE

IT may be plausibly advanced that the relation of a poet to his age should not be self-conscious, that he should neither deliberately reject the actualities, discoveries, the temper of his age, nor should he constitute himself their interpreter. The former was the error of the Romantic *à outrance*, the latter the error of the *Futuristi* and other schools and individuals now forgotten or obscure. But the Romantic attitude, even in excess, is more tolerable and less harmful because the material of poetry remains much the same in all ages and because it is almost impossible for any man to remain quite untouched by the fresh ideas current in his time. The poet, then, does not constitute himself the " interpreter of his age " ; he will draw his themes and perhaps his form from remoter times, but since he cannot escape, and ought not to wish to escape, the " spirit of his time," his work will be an expression of that spirit, according to his powers of intelligent comprehension and digestion.

He will not to-day set out to versify as much as he can understand of Einstein, he will not compose " poems of Relativity," but the mere fact that he possesses this new knowledge will make him different from predecessors who had it not, and to that extent, but no more, will he " interpret his age."

The present age is one of ferment and incoherence, not a depressing and terrifying spectacle as some imagine, but rather a heartening symptom that we are reacting against the spiritual enemies of our race—stagnation and decay—and that we are attempting to assimilate many new ideas and to bring them into order and harmony. But that the age is incoherent (perhaps all ages seem incoherent to those who live in them and need the perspective of time for their hidden order to appear luminously) is no reason why art generally, or that branch of art which we call poetry, should be incoherent. A little of the poetry written in English, a good deal of French poetry, and (if I am not misinformed) still more of German poetry, are now distinctly incoherent. On the other hand, a large proportion of recent poetry, particularly English, is stagnant, a repetition in a degraded form of something that has been done better before. The reader is in both cases disappointed ; he feels that there is plenty of energy and intelligence and talent in the poetry I have called " incoherent,"

o   209 but it fails to become art because it lacks *ordonnance*; while he feels that the order of the poetry I have called stagnant is arbitrary, artificial, and unintelligent. The poetry which this hypothetical reader is seeking, which he is convinced can be written and will be written, has not yet emerged. Perhaps this is due largely to the erroneous conceptions of the art cherished by poets, to the fact that they have not clearly determined what is to be done, or, having determined, have arrived at a fallacious conclusion. The present time is undoubtedly rich in varied poetic talents, but the possessors of those talents seem unable to use them to the best advantage. They seem unable to put into their poetry all the fine things that are in their minds, so that it is far more interesting to listen to the conversation of modern poets (*tête-à-tête*, not in groups) than to read their poetry. Other observers must have been equally surprised that men so intelligent, so thoughtful, so sensitive, so variously informed should produce in poetry work which is so insignificant, abortive, and timid. It is perhaps over-optimistic to think so, but I believe that (Shakespeare and Donne apart) we have nearly as many able and intelligent men writing poetry now as in the first quarter of the seventeenth century.[1] Our con-

---

[1] This is certainly a preposterous statement, but I leave it as evidence, not of intelligence, but of good-will.

temporaries have a far greater stock of notions and
ideas than the Jacobean dramatists, or are more
truly refined, and have more delicate perceptions
than the lyrists ; yet they are completely unable
to compass either the abounding and vigorous
fecundity of the dramatists or the exquisite grace
and happy refinement of the song-writers. Are
they " tongue-tied by authority " ? For tongue-
tied they, we, all of us, undoubtedly are. I do not
mean that too little poetry is written (perhaps there
is rather too much), but that the poets do not put
into their poetry a hundredth part of the richness
of their natures and of the abundance of their
thoughts. Future ages, looking back on us, will
conclude that we were either amiable and peddling
or vapid and indisciplined ; that when our poetry
had order it was effete and when it had vigour it
was shapeless. I am tempted to blame all this as
much upon the ignorance, conceit, and snobbery
of audiences as upon the errors of the poets. The
point is that this age might be, and ought to be,
as rich in good secondary poetry as the Jacobean
age, yet in spite of the bulk of work produced it
is poorer in quality than that written in any of
the periods 1600–22, 1700–22, 1800–22, and only
superior to that meagre poetic age, 1500–22.

It is necessary to call a halt to this prolix digression and to return to the theme of the poet's

relation to his age. That somewhat vague expression suggests a bewildering number of lines of inquiry. One might ask, for example, why it is that certain periods have been more favourable to the production of poetry than others ; why in the age of Elizabeth it was disgraceful for a gentleman to be unable to pen a sonnet, compose a song and sing it to the lute, while in the age of George V no gentleman would be guilty of such acts, and a poet is held to be a slightly ludicrous, if not ignominious figure. One might also investigate the relation between the arts and sciences, their analogies and differences, their apparent hostility. Or again, one might contrast the conception of poetry held by a writer in the age of Dante (when the " noble " topics for a poet were held to be War, Love, and God) with the conception which a contemporary might have, seeing that we consider War disgusting and barbarous, that our theories of Love are largely physiological (we have all read Freud and Mr. Ellis), and that most of us hold that gods are made by men, not men by gods. Thus " heroic " war poetry, Petrarchan love poetry, and religious poetry, if written to-day, run the risk of appearing merely artificial or unintelligent to educated people. Retrospectively we enjoy Homer, Petrarch, and Dante, but we cannot hope to revive the heroic epic, the canzone of mystic love, or the vision of

212

hell, purgatory, and paradise. The imagination may
be just as lively now as in the thirteenth century,
but it must surely work along different lines,
from different *données*, and with a different frame-
work. The vulgar notion that science has abolished
poetry, that experiment has dispossessed the
imagination, is untenable, for science finds itself
surrounded by the mysterious. (Twice two does
not always make four—we are told—and the spectacle of a starry night which used to be propounded
as an awe-striking evidence of providential order
is now shown to present the appearance of relationships which have never existed.) But while the poet
cannot and must not take the data of science as a
theme, he ought not to be ignorant of the present
deductions of scientists. One condition of science
is that it is always being superseded, whereas art
is not superseded. I have open before me an
anonymous French song of the thirteenth century.
The man who wrote it believed in the Trinity, the
primum mobile, the diurnal motion of the sun,
and probably held that unicorns could be captured
by a pure maid ; most of us disbelieve these things,
but yet we do not find the following lines anything
but pleasurable—

> Sa bele bouche tendrete
> Que je soloie baiser,
> Qui plus estoit vermeillete
> Que la rose d'un rosier,

> Soëf con flor d'esglentier
> Getoit une savorete,
> Mès quant el ne m'a mestier,
> Trop me semble mès fadete,
> Et son cler vis
> Mi semble descolorés et frois et paliz.

What do we conclude from this? Simply that though science has altered completely since 1300, art has merely developed. The science of 1300 is now tedious and quaint; its art is still enjoyable. Yet we must not conclude that the modern poet stands in exactly the same relation to his art as the mediæval *chansonnier*; he may undergo the same experience, but it will affect him differently and be expressed differently. Here, for example, is the modern *chansonnier* on the same theme—

> T'aimer, c'est beaucoup trop complexe
> pour un poème. Affaire d'sexe
> et d'âme et d'sexe et d'â . . . Mais les
> Oh! les femmes qu'on vexe!
> —Je sens, chère, que tu me hais.

I shall not be so bold as to say that M. Pellerin's little poem will be as enjoyable in 2522 as the mediæval song is in 1922; it is an example of that unhappy incoherence I have been lamenting: but the two citations are at once a proof of the statement that the material of poetry remains the same and of the argument that the attitude of the poet, and hence his treatment of the material, must

214

change. Heaven forbid that I should attribute to
M. Pellerin's little piece a profundity he never intended, yet I think it no straining of truth to say
that the attitude implied is harmonious with that
expressed by him elsewhere, when he calls the human
race a " dérisoire unité dans l'immensité plané-
taire "—a modern conception which was obviously
impossible to the mediæval poet. I feel (if this is
not spinning too finely) that the earlier poet is more
comfortable and serene in his clockwork universe,
wound up and kept running by an anthropomorphic
God, than the modern poet who is tortured by a
sense of human insignificance, by the frailty and
brevity of all human affairs, and disturbed by the
colossal enigmas involved in our conceptions of
the universe. In this way and this way only does
science influence the arts, in this way only can we
admit " modernity " in poetry.

The instinct which has prevented most English
poets of this age from running after Marinetti, to
praise motor-cars, or to grow hysterical over aero-
planes, seems to me in this respect healthy and
admirable. It is worth recalling that themes of a
similar kind were set by the French Academy for
poets in the mechanical delirium which accom-
panied the promotion of railways ; all these works
are now utterly forgotten.

There is much in Arnold's 1853 preface to his

poems which appears debatable, particularly his
insistence upon the purely classical idea of "noble
actions" as essentials to poetry.[1] Nevertheless,
there is great wisdom for us in his words, and we
ought to weigh them carefully. I am particularly
reminded of this preface in reading modern American poetry and criticism and, to a lesser extent,
modern French and Italian poetry, particularly
that of the Unanimistes (so called), of Apollinaire
and his pupils, and Marinetti and his pupils. The
passage I mean runs as follows—

> They do not talk of their mission, nor of interpreting their
> age, nor of the coming poet ; all this, they know, is the mere
> delirium of vanity ; their business is not to praise their age, but
> to afford to the men who live in it the highest pleasure they
> are capable of feeling. If asked to afford this by means of
> subjects drawn from the age itself, they ask what special fitness
> the age has for supplying them : they are told that it is an era of
> progress, an age commissioned to carry out the great ideas of
> industrial development and social amelioration. They reply
> that with all this they can do nothing ; that the elements
> they need for the exercise of their art are great actions, calcu-
> lated powerfully and delightfully to affect what is permanent
> in the human soul ; that so far as the present age can supply
> such actions, they will gladly make use of them ; but that
> an age wanting in moral grandeur can with difficulty supply
> such, and an age of spiritual discomfort with difficulty be
> powerfully and delightfully affected by them.

That, I think, effectually disposes of the wild west
and aeroplane schools. Yet, lest by applauding

[1] Thus eliminating "personal poetry," like much of that written
by Heine, Donne, and Verlaine.

that passage I should seem to approve other writers who are defective in a different way, I may point out that we cannot give the men who live in this age "the highest pleasure they are capable of" by—the words are Johnson's—" descriptions copied from descriptions, by imitations borrowed from imitations, by traditional imagery and hereditary similes, by readiness of rhyme and volubility of syllables."

In reflecting on another of the points touched upon, the relation of the contemporary poet to his audience, I feel, as I said before, tempted to blame the audience as much as the poet for the comparative ineffectiveness of our present poetic literature. It is impossible to deny that the artist is influenced by his audience. Even the sternest and most complacent self-critic must be a little moved by the reception of his works. I cannot altogether accept the proposal that the poet should write for "one hypothetical intelligent reader," because such cynicism wounds me and because poetry so written runs grave risks of becoming too allusive and refined, unintelligible and uninteresting to all but the author and his immediate circle. It is class poetry, not national poetry—and how limited the class which consists of one hypothetical individual! And I am equally unable to accept the romantic conception of the "poète incompris," who sacrifices himself for a problematical posterity and solaces himself by reflecting upon his post-humous immortality. The classic examples of the " poète incompris " are either men who died very young or men who created an insurmountable pre-judice against their names by excessive arrogance, eccentricity, or vice. Moreover, I do not know of any poets of marked ability who lived to the age of forty without receiving some sympathy and encouragement from competent judges. The quarrel I would lay upon the present English audience of poetry-readers, to whom in the first place a contemporary poet must naturally address himself for censure or approval, is that this audience is not very competent even at its best, that it applauds in new poetry precisely those vices of imitation and emptiness which Johnson so vigor-ously denounced. In other words, a writer who imitates skilfully some of the more popular of our poets—say Keats or Wordsworth—is more likely to be encouraged and applauded than the far more valuable, if more austere, poet described by Arnold. Popular authors sometimes complain that the public pins them down to one particular kind of book. " Disregard the public " is the immediate retort equally of the romantic and of the proud intellectual, but it seems to me (I may be wrong) that the poet injures himself when he " disregards

the public " too obtrusively and too arrogantly.
I cannot escape from the certainty that poetry is
to give pleasure ; and if it is giving pleasure to
nobody, or to one hypothetical individual only,
I see no reason for making it public. Probably
it would be an advantage if poets generally published their poems first in periodicals (this is easy
enough) and forebore to issue them in book form
until they were convinced that enough people wanted
them, to justify publication. (I hope it is no great
cynicism to say that the criticism a book of poetry
receives from the press is usually so perfunctory
and unintelligent that it is not of the slightest value
to the writer.) But, just as I would exhort the
poets to make every effort to render themselves
capable of giving " the highest pleasure " to their
readers, so I would exhort their readers to be certain that what they ask from contemporary poets
is truly the " highest pleasure " of original creation
and not the comparatively base pleasure of skilful
imitation. " On se lasse de parler dans un ouate,"
says Claudel, speaking of the complete silence which
met his early books. I do not believe that there
is any contemporary English poet of even slight
merit who has not received encouragement, perhaps
more than he deserves ; there is probably more
danger that a good imitative poet will be over-
praised than neglected ; but as much cannot be

said of the exceptional and original poet—one reflects how long Mr. Doughty's poetry lay in oblivion, and wonders if the "Dynasts" would have been so readily accepted had Mr. Hardy not previously been known by his novels. In other words, I feel that the readers of poetry in England are in a state of mind common to many nations rich in past literature, that of applauding able variations on old work rather than genuine creation. Perhaps audiences have always been so ; at least I know that I have to struggle against the tendency in myself to prefer good imitative new poetry to more original and hence more disconcerting work. Moreover, the almost inexhaustible mass of existing good poetry is a great temptation to neglect the more speculative pleasures of contemporary work. It is so easy to feel that one must not read Mr. Blunden now, because one is still ignorant of Clare and Bloomfield. Nevertheless, good contemporary poetry has an interest for us which it can never have for later generations, and we are thoroughly unwise and unintelligent if we take the rash stand that there is no good contemporary poetry. There is ; but may we not exhort the poets to strive to make their poetry still more capable of giving "the highest pleasure " ? And, as the poet's audience, ought we not to be careful that we do not esteem that which is less excellent above that which is more excellent ?

I do not know that any precept or recipes for perfection can be extracted from these divagations. I come back to my conviction, or rather feeling, that the poets of this generation, though rich enough in talent, well endowed spiritually and intellectually, have not yet been able to develop more than a fraction of their poetical potentialities. It is as if they acquiesced in the vulgar or popular novelist's view that poetry is a kind of genial but unimportant game of a traditional kind, best left in the hands of amateurs and amiable dilettanti. It is as if the poets had deliberately starved their art, condemned it to the malnutrition of a perpetual imitation, not of life, but of itself. Yet it may be safely asserted that poetry is the most durable, valuable, and pleasure-giving part of literature, that he who is insensible to poetry is defective in taste and incapable of experiencing the greatest pleasures which literature can give. The achievements of English poets in the past are so various, so considerable, and so delightful that we might be pardoned if, as a race, we ceased to produce any more poetry of the first class or even of the good second class. The past two or three decades seem to us comparatively barren; but they may not appear so in the future; and, in any event, no race can produce a continual stream of masterpieces. There must be periods of repose as well as periods of production. In English literature it is generally the unexpected which happens, and (who knows ?) the next generation may see another outburst of poetry equal to that of the first quarter of the seventeenth and nineteenth centuries. But in any event there is no need to despair ; the present generation has at least handed on the torch ; and a little more ardour and enterprise in the poets, a little more enthusiasm and discrimination in their audience, might create the rich period which we hope for rather than expect.

XX

ET EGO IN ARCADIA

THE Italian pastoral is like Italian wine: it
does not travel well, but in its own climate
is delicious. To enjoy fully the "Orfeo" and the
"Aminta" in England is difficult, for these delicate
pieces address themselves to a particular mood,
achieve their effect through the reader's having
been prepared to receive it by influences of climate
and the plastic arts. This note will do no more
than dwell upon the pleasures of reading in Italy the
works of Poliziano, Tasso, and Guarini; assuredly
it will not advocate a revival of pastoral drama.

The word "pastoral" is generally applied to
anything written about the country and country
people, and thus is forced to cover the most diverse
types—the wild, snub-nosed goatherds of Theocritus,
the scented creations of the Marquis de Racan, and
Mr. Hardy's positivist hinds. This opens the net
too wide. All true pastoral, including the drama,
is marked by the following features—

1. A more or less idealized country life.

2. Some classical machinery of Arcadian or mytho-
   logical personages, *dii familiares*, Pucks, and
   what-not.
3. *Cortesìa* or *amour courtois*, ranging from mere
   exaggeration of sentiment to fantastic chivalry.
4. A preoccupation with and influence from the
   arts of sculpture, painting, and architecture.

The genre is peculiarly Italian, though Greek
genius, origin of nearly all European art, has given
it strong characteristics. So dependent is pastoral
upon the classical background that it rarely pleases
those who do not like the classics. In fact, Renaissance pastoral is quite generally definable as the
dream of a Hellenic earthly paradise created by the
eternal sense of exile in those who love beauty.
The modern cult of what is childish and quaint
may be a perversion of the same sentiment, like
all political millenniarism ; but how much more
prudent to gratify this instinct in avowed fictions
than to attempt to carry it into life !

The Renaissance pastoral play, which came after
the pastoral novel of Sannazaro (not such a bad
poet) is founded principally upon Theocritus, Virgil,
and Longus. There are multitudes of other sources
and influences, but to attempt any general sketch
of pastoral is far beyond my powers or the scope of
an article. All I wish to assert is : That, in the
Cinquecento, pastoral was a complex and allusive art,

addressed to a polished and frequently learned audience, with whom it was extremely popular. The Renaissance eclogue is held to be tiresome— the official word is " artificial," though curiously enough " inartificial " is also a word of disparagement. I confess I am not so difficult. I like to read in faultless Italian or tasteful (and easy) neo-Latin how Napæa left her flock at the hottest of the day to lie beneath a " sun-warding " beech, while Alexis sang to the music of the pipe and rippling waters and the gods rustled among the myrtles. I should not try to put this imaginary perfection into practice during an English winter, or even summer, but I cannot forbear adding that at the end of a day's work I prefer to sleep upon such images than upon thoughts of the eternal dreary couple in the same grimy street presented in the same gritty style. There is a sort of hebetude in both tastes, but the workmanship of the poets as well as their subject is more delightful than that of the pseudo-realists. It is pleasant to feel one shares this taste with Coleridge, for somewhere in the " Biographia " he bursts into a long note on the Strozzi and Cinquecento poetry, which note proves that he understood this, as he understood every other, kind of literary pleasure, and is itself the most intelligent analysis of the genre I have seen in modern criticism.

LITERARY STUDIES AND REVIEWS

It is interesting to see how different nations treated the pastoral. The Italians soon brought it to a perfect formalism, in which the reader is simply to admire the virtuosity of the poet in performing regular variations upon fixed themes. In Spain (we are told) it ran to honour and chivalry and noble chimeras. In France it cultivated superficial good manners, grew epigrammatic, but was never much liked. In England it was heroical with Sidney, charming with Spenser, a little flat with the eclogue-writers of the Davison's Poetical Rhapsody kind, but then was happily taken up by the dramatists, from Shakespeare, who used it perfectly as subsidiary to his main action, to Randolph and other minor writers. The experts generally concede that the best pastoral plays are the English and the Italian. The difference of treatment is remarkable. The Italians were very serious about their Arcadian machinery; obviously the mere use of it gave them a voluptuous æsthetic delight. A line of verse like

E Pane e Palla e Priapo e Pomona

no doubt hit them with a pleasure our less sensitive and less prepared minds cannot experience. And they worked out their themes as strictly as a fugue. The English cared little about this machinery. Their Arcadia was the country near Stratford, round

about Grace-Dieu or Rye or even Richmond. They
minimized, because they did not understand the
cortesìa, which Shakespeare even made fun of in
" As You Like It." Some of them, with Peele, were
not a little bawdy. The audience of the "Aminta,"
though doubtless more " corrupt " than the people
who listened to " The Old Wives' Tale," were too
well-bred, too " correct " in taste to allow bawdy
in pastoral. In satire or Terentian comedy as
much bawdy as the author could compass, but not
in pastoral. The objection was, of course, not
moral but æsthetic. At least one reason for the
diminishing appreciation of Renaissance art—the
growth, in fact, of a positive hostility to it—is
that to the Renaissance man beauty meant a great
deal, and to the modern man it means almost nothing.
In the sixteenth century the hostlers were critics
of art and literature; the position now appears to
be reversed. So many people, one feels, do not
know what is meant by " beauty," misapply the
word to objects which have little or no relation to
beauty. This may be part of the new barbarism
into which we are supposed to be falling; but even
new barbarians need not allow themselves to be
fubbed off with theories which amount to saying
that beauty is that which is never beautiful. Even
if we have (very reluctantly) to give up the Platonic
conception of absolute beauty, if we admit that

227

" beauty " does not exist but only beautiful objects, if, therefore, we have to make the dangerous admission that beauty is a relative quality; even then, that furnishes no reason for applying the term to objects which do not possess the quality at all. Now, the Italian pastoral plays are saturated with this Renaissance obsession with beauty. It is scarcely incorrect to say that so long as his work had the desired "morbidezza," the Cinquecento artist let almost everything else go. Undoubtedly this is an artistic error which seriously affected later Italian art of all kinds, but it means that whatever other faults Cinquecento work has, it has the virtue of being beautiful. And—if I may continue this digression—whatever virtues contemporary work has, very little of it is beautiful. This generation is afraid of beauty, is afraid to admit publicly that it loves beauty. That is the result partly of the æsthetic surfeit of the eighties and nineties, partly of the fate of the contemptible Oscar Wilde, and partly of beauty's degradation into prettiness at the hands of stupid or unprincipled purveyors of middle-class " art." Moreover, beautiful objects have become common through photographic reproduction, tourist facilities, the machinations of tourist agencies and uplifters of the people generally. But this is a detestable form of snobbery—to avoid beauty, to cultivate a dislike for beautiful things,

228

because a conventional (and hypocritical) appreciation of them is common. Really, those who are
so shy of beauty need have no fear ; to care deeply
and intelligently for beautiful things is still rather
uncommon. I once heard an intellectual snob
discourse of the " sentimentalism and prettiness of
Pheidias." I often wonder if he knew that no
truly authentic work of Pheidias exists, and whether
most of the depreciation of beautiful things we
hear is equally solidly based upon knowledge and
intelligence ? Perhaps the modern horror of
pastoral rests on the same kind of inverted
snobbery ?

The " Orfeo " of Poliziano is said to be the parent
of opera. If so, it has had a curiously mixed progeny.
Perhaps it did set the fashion for masks. I read
somewhere a statement that the mask began with the
" Orfeo " and ended with " Comus." But the mask
did not end with " Comus " ; it merely divorced itself
from poetry at some period after that fruitful liaison
with the puritan muse. For what are Russian
ballets but sophisticated developments of the mask,
from which music and decoration have expelled any
literary pleasure ? The " Orfeo " differs from the
pastoral plays of Tasso and Guarini and offers some
suggestive analogies to the masks of Ben Jonson.
Poliziano was a Quattrocento Florentine in feeling.
His mask is, of course, in exquisite taste, but it

does possess Florentine vitality and realism as well as Florentine humanism. The songs " Non ti fuggir, donzella " and " Udite, selve, mie dolce parole " are in their own way as good as Ben Jonson's and beautifully turned. The shepherd scene (" Avresti visto un mio vitellin bianco ") is more a copying of life than similar scenes in the " Pastor Fido " and " Aminta," but does suggest the realistic strokes of English pastoral. One version of the " Orfeo " (there are two texts) includes some pleasant neo-Latin sapphics, a violation of the unity of language which would have shocked the Cinquecento. The final song " Ognun segua, Bacco, te," is related to the Florentine carnival songs, whereas the lyric parts of " Aminta " and " Pastor Fido " are a development of classical chorus. The " Orfeo " is therefore a far less stately and formal business than the later pastoral. If it be pedantic, it has the generous pedantry of enthusiasm, not the cold pedantry of formal fops.

The fable was the weak part of pastoral drama. In the mask the fable was intentionally made subordinate to the songs and dancing and costume ; we accept its weakness as a convention. Poliziano and Ben Jonson avoided the evil consequences of a poor architecture by rapid change of scene and costume and interpolated song and dance ; Shakespeare solved the difficulty by weaving his pastoral scenes

into a play which possessed some other action
to interest the audience. The unfinished " Sad
Shepherd " of Ben Jonson was meant to be a new
development of pastoral, and it recognized this
architectural weakness by introducing popular
" features " like witchcraft and Robin Hood, and
Maid Marian. But the whole-hearted pastoral play,
whether it be " Aminta " or " The Faithful
Shepherdess " or " Les Bergeries " suffers badly
from this defect. In fact, the pastoral play must be
unsatisfactory as a dramatic spectacle, even when
trimmed with music and dancing. At its best it
is a series of set pieces, bearing some relation to
each other, but practically complete in themselves.
The pastoral play is therefore open to the fatal
objection that the whole is less important than the
parts. I have never read the whole of the " Pastor
Fido " straight through, and I believe I should find
myself tip-toeing out about the middle of the third
act of any complete performance of the play. But
when high critical *dicta* interrupt our enjoyment
of beauty, may we not occasionally let them slip ?
The best parts of pastoral drama are so beautiful,
are such delicate poetry, that I shall fight furiously
against any critic who tries to wean or threaten
me from my pleasure in this not quite first-rate
literature. In fact, I think it a mistake to discourage
a taste for good work of the second order, if only

for the tactical reason that even the best work of the present period can only claim attention on that category. On the other hand, we have to admit that one great weakness of modern poetic drama is precisely this architectural defect so apparent in the Renaissance pastoral.

There is one contrast between the Italian and the English pastoral strongly indicative of national habits. That is the attitude to sex. The Italians, without ever being bawdy, are full-flushed and sensual. The English are puritanical. In the " Aminta " the "inevitable Satyr "—as some French cynic calls it —openly asserts his intention of possessing Silvia by violence, and seems to expect the audience to concur. In " The Faithful Shepherdess " the Satyr is stricken into supernatural respect for Clorin's chastity. " Comus " is a paneygyric of the virtue which, as Renan says somewhere, " is of no importance to Nature." That Lamb felt it necessary to deprecate the character of Chloe, the wanton shepherdess, is one more evidence of this prudery. Fletcher is never happy in his characterization of passionate women ; he seems to have held the crude notion that women are either " honest " or " whores." In this respect Dryden's treatment of Cleopatra is more indulgent than Shakespeare's. Fletcher's Chloe is a poor imitation of Guarini's Corisca. In spite of her wig, Corisca has emotions where Chloe appears only to endure imperious sensations. Thus Chloe laments—

> Is it not strange, among so many a score
> Of lusty bloods, I should pick out these things,
> Whose veins, like a dull river far from springs,
> Is still the same, slow, heavy and unfit
> For stream or motion, though the strong winds hit
> With their continual power upon his sides ?
> Oh, happy be your names that have been brides,
> And tasted those rare sweets for which I pine !
> And far more heavy be thy grief and tine,
> Thou lazy swain, that mayst relieve my needs,
> Than his, upon whose liver always feeds
> A hungry vulture.

That is both coarse and clumsy, the essentially puritan idea of " wickedness." Compare those lines with Aminta's description of his first kissing Silvia, or almost any of the numerous love passages in " Il Pastor Fido." The sentiment is exaggerated from our point of view, but it is not so much a sentimental affectation as a later development of "cortesìa," which had become sensual while remaining poetical and refined. This is no doubt a degeneration. It is a painful descent from Dante's dignified

> La bocca mi baciò tutto tremante,

to Tasso's

> La semplicetta Silvia, . .
> . . . fece
> Più cupa e più mortale
> La mia piaga verace,

233

Quando le labbra sue
Giunse a le labbra mie.
Nè l'api d'alcun fiore
Coglionsì dolce il succo
Come fu dolce il mel ch' allora io colsi
Da quelle fresche rose ;
Se ben gli ardenti baci,
Che spingeva il desire a inumidirsi,
Raffrenò la temenza,
E la vergogna, e fèlli
Più lenti e meno audaci.
Ma mentre al cor scendeva
Quella dolcezza, mista
D'un secreto veleno,
Tal diletto n'avea,
Che . . . etc.

Admittedly much Cinquecento poetry is little more than a dilution of Petrarch and the classics ; admittedly north of the Alps such work has an excess of sweetness that is not always pleasing. Nevertheless, in Italy it is exactly the right literary companion for a flask of Aleatico or Montefiascone —wines which are probably intolerable when carried from their native soil. This admission exposes an unguarded flank, but I protest it was not the wine alone ; though in a wine-drinking country art is not always such a peevish and improving function as it tends to become in puritan countries. Moreover, there is the important influence of climate, and the still more important influence of the plastic arts. To enjoy once more Italian sunlight and

234

art after a long period of hyperborean existence is
suddenly to discover one had been suffering spiritual
starvation without knowing it. Sculpture becomes
very important ; painting sheds all the futile theories
it has acquired in Paris and becomes a pleasure
again instead of a series of painful intellectual feats ;
architecture speaks a hundred beautiful and interesting things instead of gabbling dully : " Money,
money, money." After seeing few beautiful objects
for years, one sees many beautiful objects in a few
weeks. The result of this is a triple intoxication ;
one roams in a golden dream of beauty, none the
less real because it exists neither for the average
resident nor the average tourist. The mind appre-
hends the world plastically ; beautiful form and
colour confer intense meaning and pleasure. To
such a mood Cinquecento poetry responds with
more facility than the nobler austerities of Dante ;
its very weaknesses are seductive. Above all, the
" set pieces " of the pastoral plays, those bas-reliefs
in words, are enchanting ; there is a sensual enjoyment in merely reading beautiful words beautifully
arranged, in contemplating some merely charming
group sketched in conventionally lovely phrases by
a delicate artist. Take these lines—

> Essendo io fanciulletto, sì che a pena
> Giunger potea con la man pargoletta

A corre i frutti da i piegati rami
De gli arboscelli, intrinseco divenni
De la più vaga e cara verginella
Che mai spiegasse al vento chioma d'oro.

The last two lines are especially beautiful. That
they are borrowed from Virgil and Petrarch is no
disparagement, because Cinquecento poetry believed
in borrowing beauties, was free from our chimeras
of unique personal originality. The Italians have a
gift for building new beauties with the ruins of
old. Strangely enough, the most fascinating period
of English poetry is that in which the poets borrowed
most extensively from abroad, particularly from
Italy. Those two lines put into English have a
very Elizabethan ring. We do not always realize
how extensively our poets from Spenser to Milton
were indebted to the Italians. Milton's style is
remarkably Italianate. I am ignorant of modern
criticism of Milton, so I may be knocking down
open doors, but I feel he is more indebted to Italian
imitators of the classics than even to the classics
themselves. Lycidas has long seemed to me a
skilful reproduction of the neo-Latin elegy of the
Navagero, Castiglioni, and Bembo type. Milton
invigorates and improves upon them, but they
were his masters as much as Virgil. The very faults
of Lycidas are Italian. The more stately style of
" Comus " has considerable affinity with that of

Guarini. Look, for example, at the opening of the Prologue to the " Pastor Fido "—

> Se per antica, e forse
> Da voi negletta e non creduta fama,
> Avete mai d'innamorato Fiume
> Le maraviglie udite,
> Che, per seguir l'onda fugace e schiva
> Dell' amata Aretusa
> Corse (o forza d'Amor) le più profonde
> Viscere della terra
> E del mar, penetrando
> Là dove sotto alla gran mole etnea,
> Non so se fulminato o fulminante,
> Vibra il fiero Gigante
> Contra 'l nemico ciel fiamme di sdegno . . .

The resemblance is curious. But Milton is an abstract poet compared with Tasso ; he takes no pleasure in elegant picture-making and conceits. Among all this lively image-worshipping Milton is a sort of Semitic iconoclast. Tasso lingers over his pictures with infinite complacence, and the sound of his lines is indeed " linkéd sweetness long drawn out." Guarini is even more affectionately verbose. Few poets equal Tasso for effects of voluptuous charm—

> Mira là quel colombo
> Con che dolce susurro lusingando
> Bacia la sua compagna ;
> Odi quel lusignuolo
> Che va di ramo in ramo
> Cantanto : *Io amo, io amo*. . . .

The suave period continues its leisurely music for line after line of phraseology, felicitous and delightful. Given the right mood of receptivity, such poetry is eminently pleasurable. Even when Guarini expands into thirty-five lines the nine lines of Catullus—

> Ut flos in septis secretus nascitur hortis . . .

one does not protest, though conscious that a contemporary would hardly receive such indulgence.

The English poets triumph over the Italian pastoral dramatists chiefly in their appreciation of "nature." The Italians like out-of-doors scenes carefully arranged and trimmed. But one should avoid the mistake of calling even this arranged pastoral scenery unnatural and "artificial"; many a description to which those words are carelessly applied is true enough to southern country. How often we hear Theocritus called "artificial," when the idylls are saturated with the country life of southern Italy. The Cinquecento poets are æsthetic, not romantic, but seeing they work from different surroundings with rather more refined taste, I cannot perceive that they are any less "natural" than their English successors. True, the looser English method has its compensations. "The Faithful Shepherdess" is deeply influenced by Italian poetry, but—it may be fancy—I find something very fresh and pellucid in this passage, one which it is pleasant

to think may have suggested to Keats the theme of
" Endymion "—

> Shepherd, I pray thee stay.   Where has thou been ?
> Or whither goest thou ?   Here be woods as green
> As any ; air likewise as fresh and sweet
> As where smooth Zephyrus plays on the fleet
> Face of the curled streams ; with flowers as many
> As the young spring gives, and as choice as any ;
> Here be all new delights, cool streams and wells,
> Arbours o'ergrown with woodbines, caves and dells ;
> Choose where thou wilt, whilst I sit by and sing,
> Or gather rushes, to make many a ring
> For thy long fingers ; tell thee tales of love,
> How the pale Phœbe, hunting in a grove,
> First saw the boy Endymion, from whose eyes
> She took eternal fire that never dies ;
> How she conveyed him softly in a sleep,
> His temples bound with poppy, to the steep
> Head of old Latmus, where she stoops each night,
> Gilding the mountain with her brother's light,
> To kiss her sweetest.

I have no moral, critical or otherwise, to insinuate
except that I find these poets a pleasant emollient
after the spiritual exacerbation induced by French
poets and English novelists. It is perhaps useful
to remind oneself that there are many kinds of
excellence even in poetry. I do not think this a
good time to write pastoral poetry, but it is rather
a good time to read it. One cannot live on Baude-
laire and James Joyce alone. We have had plenty
of sordid horrors shot at us in the last five years ;

239

I confess I am a little tired of them and of the intellectualism which appears to be largely a reaction against popular sentimentalism. If the age is a dirty age and a flabby age we must, of course, allow the satirists and the naturalists and the moralists to perform their functions. But we are not all dirty and flabby. And there are times when the high intellectual pose is as repulsive and irritating as the high intellectual voice—how well one knows it! Therefore, O Pan and all you other deathless gods, grant me

> Umbræ frigidulæ, arborum susurri,
> Antra roscida, discolore picta
> Tellus gramine, fontium loquaces
> Lymphæ, garrulæ aves, amica Musis
> Otia . . .

XXI

THEOCRITUS IN CAPRI

WE have all a few nooks of enchantment in our memories to turn back to for consolation and pleasure. In the creation of them perhaps more depended upon the inner man than upon outward events ; the determination to find beauty and at least momentary happiness will find some satisfaction almost everywhere. Youth, spring in a Mediterranean island, Greek poetry, idleness—these were the simple factors of an enchantment whose memory will only end with life. It was of no importance that youth was qualified by penury, that the spring was a mere phenomenon, the result of sidereal motions, that the island was the tourist-ridden Capri and the Greek poet—Theocritus—had never attempted to describe it. Such contingencies have no effect upon a happily constituted mind.

Those were the days when Greek was an intoxication of delight, when there was no need to " have Saint Praxed's ear," for the imagination supplied all things needful, when the white violet was peculiarly sacred and gained a new mysterious beauty because it was the flower of Meleager, when a plane-tree was not a botanical object, but the platanos, the broad, rustling foliage in whose shade Plato talked with Phædrus of divine love. Under the whispering pine on the scarped and flower-scented side of Monte Solaro, with the vast sailless Tyrrhenian like a deeper sky beneath, with Pæstum far away on the one hand, Baiæ on the other, and light foam about the islands of the Sirens (" Hither to us, great heart of the Achæans ! "); all the mechanical effort and pride of the modern world were as nothing.

To make all things perfect, to express that beauty from which the modern shrinks and for which his speech is harsh and inadequate, came the revelation of Theocritus—no poet of artifice and facile glamour, as base men declare, but one who loved beauty, the mingled austerity and richness of these southern rocks in their light garment of flowers. Even in the miniature Sicily of Capri—with Vesuvius for Ætna—it was apparent that Theocritus had exquisitely keen sensibility to all that was lovely about him. And since there is no language but Greek which can bring ecstasy into measure, which can be at once rich in feeling and austere in expression, Theocritus is for ever a great interpreter of this kind of beauty. Hundreds have kindled at his flame, but none, not even Virgil, has the power to communicate the same rapture with such perfection. And yet so strong is that first charm that even the feeblest repetition of that song by the most diffuse Italian imitator has its answer in us because we know that he too has felt this rush, this élan of happiness—

Fuggite omai, pensier' noiosi e foschi,
Che fatto avete a me sì lunga sera ;
Ch'io vo' cercar le apriche e liete piagge,
Prendendo in su l'erbette un dolce sonno ;
Perchè so ch'uom mai fatto di terra
Più felice di me non vide il sole.

Now, if we ask about happiness they tell us that labour is happiness, or they speak vaguely of women or suggest prostration before the idol of Social Service, whose real name is Busybody. But then we were happy, then we were near the gods, then we knew our lady of wisdom in her virgin house of marble, our lord of Delos, who is sun and song, and many lesser gods of hills, trees, and the sea verge, whose voices we heard in the noon silence, whose forms we saw in the twilight flitting silently and uncertainly among dark trees or gleaming from the breaking waves. And by Theocritus we learned to see them.

How much to be learned of truth and beauty from that first idyll alone where Thyrsis and the Goatherd sing ! True, the poet spoke of the murmur of falling waters, and there are no streams in Capri, but he taught us to hear and to understand the incommunicable song of the pine, to fear Pan, and to be hushed for his noon sleep when even the cicadas are silent; to feel the beauty of the crisp, carved wine cups, the gold tendrils of the ivy about the rim, the lovers embossed on its inner curve, and the old man who " seemed to fish with all the strength of his limbs," and the vineyard with the grapes and the little foxes. Then we saw Daphnis dying, visited by the gods, and heard the farewell to Arethusa and the prayer to Pan. And with the Goatherd we prayed that the mouth of Thyrsis might be filled with honey, for his song was sweeter than that of the cicadas. All that the poet spoke of we saw about us. There were wild pear-trees in blossom, the green-silver olive gardens, the bees murmuring in the ivy and fern as once by the cave of Amaryllis, rock-cistus and asphodel, white violets or stars of Bethlehem (whichever were Leukoïa), from which the shepherds wove their flower-crowns. In the damp recesses of the rocks were scented wild narcissus and sometimes little cyclamen flowers. There were purple anemones, the flower perhaps which sprang from the blood of Adonis. The gold and green lizards darted over the sunny rocks, the cicadas were seldom silent, the goats clambered on the rough walls and on peaks of rock, the grasshopper whirred up; the air was scented with honey. Strangest of all

244

came from close at hand the shrill, clear, pure note of a reed-pipe, made by one of the boys who guard the goats, who had been sitting silent in a little grove for hours. It was as if Lacon and Daphnis were not dead, but still making music for Pan. Two thousand years slipped from the world—" and to me there piped two shepherd lads "—beauty was truth, truth beauty.

Coming home, watching the first gleam of the evening star, Bion's " gold light of the lovely foam-born," while the sea vanished into shadow and the distant mountain grew dark swallow-blue (like Sappho's " dwelling of Persephone "), the mood did not vanish nor the happiness fail. It was an enchantment, a plenitude of beauty sufficient to sweeten much bitterness, though, like all enchantment and all beauty, it faded too soon into the past.

INDEX OF PROPER NAMES

INDEX OF PROPER NAMES

c

INDEX OF PROPER NAMES

LITERARY STUDIES AND REVIEWS

INDEX OF PROPER NAMES